THE

PROPHECIES

OF THE

BRAHAN SEER

(COINNEACH ODHAR FIOSAICHE)

BY

ALEXANDER MACKENZIE, F.S.A.Scot.

INTRODUCTORY CHAPTER

BY

ANDREW LANG

ENEAS MACKAY
STIRLING

Current impression - *1953*

Printed at the Observer Press, Stirling

CONTENTS

The Brahan Seer and Second Sight

By Andrew Lang.

―――――

Mr. Mackay has asked me to make a few comments on Mr. Mackenzie's "Prophecies of the Brahan Seer," and I do so for the sake of old times and old ideas. Unlike Mr. Mackenzie, I can unblushingly confess the belief that there probably are occasional instances of second sight, that is, of "premonitions." I know too many examples among persons of my acquaintance, mostly Lowlanders or English, to have any doubt about the matter. Hegel was of the same opinion, and was not ashamed to include second sight in his vast philosophic system.* As to the *modus* of second sight, "how it is done," in fact, I have no theory. If there is a psychical element in man, if there is something more than a mechanical result of physical processes in nerve, brain, and blood, then we cannot set any limit to the range of "knowledge supernormally acquired." "Time and space are only hallucinations," as a philosopher has audaciously remarked. They may be transcended by the spirit in man, *et voila pourquoi votre fille est muette !* This explanation, of course, is of the vaguest, but I have no better to suggest.

By an odd coincidence, two cases of second sight, of

* "Philosophie der Gheistes," werke vii. 179.—Berlin, 1845

B

recent date, in the experience of an educated lady, reached me yesterday at first hand, and, as I pen these words another (knowledge of a death at a distance) comes to me from a distinguished philologist. But he thinks he was ten minutes out in his reckoning, which, allowing for difference of watches, is not much. A fourth case is from a Royal Academician, an intimate friend. He and a lady, also of my acquaintance, were being shown over a beautiful new house by the owner. My friend, in the owner's bedroom, turned pale. The lady, when they went out, asked him what ailed him. " I saw X—— " (the owner of the house) " lying dead in his bed." X—— died within a month, which would be thought fair work in the Highlands. An odder case occurred last year. On June 15, a lady, well-known to me, and in various fields of literature, told me that, calling on another lady the day before, she had seen a vision of a man, previously unknown to her, who thrust a knife into her friend's left side. I offered to bet £100 against fulfilment. In autumn my friend, again calling at the same house, met the man of her vision on the doorsteps. Entering, she found her friend dying, as her constitution did not rally after an operation on her left side, performed by the man of the vision, who was a surgeon. This is much in the Highland manner. Of the Seers here alluded to (and I might add many other modern instances in my own knowledge), only one was Celtic. For savage examples which illustrate the belief (though evidence cannot, of course, be procured with exactness), I may be permitted to refer to my " Making of Religion " (pp. 72-158). The kind of story is always the same. And the legends of St. Columba, in Adamnan, are much on a par, in many cases, with modern examples in *The*

Proceedings of the Society for Psychical Research. The uniformity of the reports argues the existence of some facts at their base.

While I am credulous to this extent, I vastly prefer modern cases, at first hand, and corroborated (as when I can swear that the lady told me of her vision before its fulfilment), to the rumours of the Brahan Seer.   We can scarcely ever, except as to the deaf Seaforth, find any evidence that the prophecies were recorded before the event.   In many cases fulfilment could only occur, either in the ancient fighting Clan society, or under its revival, to which we cannot look with much confidence. The prophecies about sheep one has no evidence to prove earlier than, say, 1770.   As to the burning of the Seer, if it really had clerical sanction, why are Kirk Sessions' Registers not brought forward as proof? Have they been examined for this purpose?   We are, in fact, dealing with poetical legend, not with evidence.

In one respect Kenneth is peculiar among Highland Seers.   He is a " Crystal-gazer," whether his " gibber " (as Australian savages call divining stones) was blue, or grey, or pearly, perforated or not.   This use of stones, usually crystals, or black stones, I have found among Australians, Tonkaways, Aztecs, Incas, Samoyeds, Polynesians, Maoris, Greeks, Egyptians, in Fez. : water, ink, or blood being also employed to stare at.   The whole topic is discussed in my book already cited, with many modern examples.   Now I do not, elsewhere, know more than one or two cases of this kind of divination in the Highlands.   The visions are usually spontaneous and uninvoked, except when the seer uses the blade-bone of a sheep.   In the interests of Folk Lore, or Psychology, or both, people who have the opportunity should record cases of the use of divining stones in the Highlands. It is even more desirable that the statements of second-sighted men (they are common enough, to my personal knowledge, in Sutherland, Lochaber, and Glencoe) *should be taken down before fulfilment*. Unless this is done, the predictions, as matter of evidence, go for nothing. We must try to discover the percentage of failures, before we can say whether the successes are not due to chance coincidence, or to misstatement, or to mere imposture. I have little or no doubt that the Ferrintosh story (told in this book) is a misconception, based on the actual calamity at Fearn, long after the Seer was dead. In fact, like Dr. Johnson, I want more evidence. He was ready to believe, but unconvinced. I am rather more credulous, but it would be very easy to upset my faith, and certainly it cannot be buttressed by vague reports on the authority of tradition. It may be urged that to inquire seriously into such things is to encourage superstition. But if inquiry merely unearthed failure and imposture, even superstition would be discouraged.

June, 1899.

THE
PROPHECIES OF THE BRAHAN SEER

COINNEACH ODHAR FIOSAICHE.

THE gift of prophecy, second-sight, or "Taibh-searachd," claimed for and believed by many to have been possessed, in an eminent degree, by Coinneach Odhar, the Brahan Seer, is one, the belief in which scientific men and others of the present day accept as unmistakable signs of looming, if not of actual insanity. We all are, or would be considered, scientific in these days. It will, therefore, scarcely be deemed prudent for any one who wishes to lay claim to the slightest modicum of common sense, to say nothing of an acquaintance with the elementary principles of science, to commit to paper his ideas on such a subject, unless he is prepared, in doing so, to follow the common horde in their all but universal scepticism.

Without committing ourselves to any specific faith on the subject, however difficult it may be to explain away what follows on strictly scientific grounds, we shall place before the reader the extraordinary predictions of the Brahan Seer. We have had slight experiences of our own, which we would hesitate to dignify by the name of second-sight. It is not, however, with our own experiences that we have at present to do, but with the "Prophecies" of Coinneach Odhar Fiosaiche. He is beyond comparison the most distinguished of all our Highland Seers, and his prophecies have been known throughout the whole country for more than two centuries. The popular faith in them has been, and still continues to be, strong and wide-spread. Sir Walter Scott, Sir Humphrey Davy, Mr. Morritt, Lockhart, and other eminent contemporaries of the " Last of the Seaforths " firmly believed in them. Many of them were well-known, and recited from generation to generation, centuries before they were fulfilled. Some of them have been fulfilled in our own day, and many are still unfulfilled.

Not so much with the view of protecting ourselves from the charge of a belief in such superstitious folly (for we would hesitate to acknowledge any such belief), but as a slight palliation for obtruding such nonsense on the public, we may point out, by the way, that the sacred writers—who are now believed by many of the would-be-considered-wise to have been behind the age, and not near so wise and far-seeing as we are—believed in second-sight, witchcraft, and other visions of a supernatural kind. But then we shall be told by our scientific friends that the Bible itself is becoming obsolete, and that it has already served its turn ; being only suited for an unenlightened age in which men like Shake-speare, Milton, Newton, Bacon, and such unscientific men could be considered distinguished. The truth is that on more important topics than the one we are now considering, the Bible is laid aside by many of our would-be-scientific lights, whenever it treats of anything beyond the puny comprehension of the minds and intellectual vision of these omniscient gentlemen. We have all grown so scientific that the mere idea of supposing anything possible which is beyond the intellectual grasp of the scientific enquirer can-not be entertained, although even he must admit, that in many cases, the greatest men in science, and the mightiest intellects, find it impossible to understand or explain away many things as to the existence of which they have no possible doubt. We even find the clergy slightly inconsistent in questions of this kind. They solemnly desire to impress us with the fact that ministering spirits hover about the couches and apartments in which the dying Christian is drawing near the close of his existence, and preparing to throw off his mortal coil; but were we to suggest the possibility of any mere human being, in any conceivable manner having had indications of the presence of these ghostly visitors, or discovering any signs or premonitions of the early departure of a relative or of an intimate friend, our heathen ideas and devious wanderings from the safe channel of clerical orthodoxy and consistent inconsistency, would be howled against, and paraded before the faithful as the grossest superstition, with an enthusiasm and relish possible only to a strait-laced ecclesiastic. Clerical inconsistency is, however, not our present theme.

Many able men have written on the Second-sight, and to some of them we shall refer in the following pages; meanwhile our purpose is to place before the reader the Prophecies of the Brahan Seer, as far as we have been able to procure them. We are informed that a considerable collection of them has been made by the late Alexander Cameron of Lochmaddy, author of the "History and Traditions of the Isle of Skye," but we were unable to discover into whose possession the manuscript found its way; we hope, however, that this reference may bring it to light.

Kenneth Mackenzie, better known as Coinneach Odhar, the Brahan Seer (according to Mr. Maclennan), was born at Baile-na-Cille, in the Parish of Uig and Island of Lews, about the beginning of the seventeenth century. Nothing particular is recorded of his early life, but when he had just entered his teens, he received a stone in the following manner, by which he could reveal the future destiny of man :—While his mother was one evening tending her cattle in a summer shieling on the side of a ridge called Cnoc-eothail, which overlooks the burying-ground of Baile-na-Cille, in Uig, she saw, about the still hour of midnight, the whole of the graves in the churchyard opening, and a vast multitude of people of every age, from the newly-born babe to the grey-haired sage, rising from their graves, and going away in every conceivable direction. In about an hour they began to return, and were all soon after back in their graves, which closed upon them as before. But, on scanning the burying-place more closely, Kenneth's mother observed one grave, near the side, still open. Being a courageous woman, she determined to ascertain the cause of this singular circumstance, so, hastening to the grave, and placing her " cuigeal " (distaff) athwart its mouth (for she had heard it said that the spirit could not enter the grave again while that instrument was upon it), she watched the result. She had not to wait long, for in a minute or two she noticed a fair lady coming in the direction of the church-yard, rushing through the air, from the north. On her arrival, the fair one addressed her thus :—" Lift thy distaff from off my grave, and let me enter my dwelling of the dead." " I shall do so," answered the other, " when you explain to me what detained you so long after your neighbours." " That you shall soon hear," the ghost replied ; " My journey was much longer than theirs—I had to go all the way to Norway." She then addressed her :—" I am a daughter of the King of Norway ; I was drowned while bathing in that country ; my body was found on the beach close to where we now stand, and I was interred in this grave. In remembrance of me, and as a small reward for your intrepidity and courage, I shall possess you of a valuable secret—go and find in yonder lake a small round blue stone, which give to your son, Kenneth, who by it shall reveal future events." She did as requested, found the stone, and gave it to her son, Kenneth. No sooner had he thus received the gift of divination than his fame spread far and wide. He was sought after by the gentry throughout the length and breadth of the land, and no special assembly of theirs was complete unless Coinneach Odhar was amongst them. Being born on the lands of Seaforth, in the Lews, he was more associated with that family than with any other in the country, and he latterly removed to the neighbour-hood of Loch Ussie, on the Brahan estate, where he worked as a common labourer on a neighbouring farm. He was very shrewd and clear-headed, for one in his menial position; was always ready with a smart answer, and if any attempted to raise the laugh at his expense, seldom or ever did he fail to turn it against his tormentors.

There are various other versions of the manner in which he became possessed of the power of divination. According to one—His mistress, the farmer's wife, was unusually exacting with him, and he, in return, continually teased, and, on many occasions, expended much of his natural wit upon her, much to her annoyance and chagrin. Latterly, his conduct became so unbearable that she decided upon disposing of him in a manner which would save her any future annoyance. On one occasion, his master having sent him away to cut peats, which in those days were, as they now are in more remote districts, the common article of fuel, it was necessary to send him his dinner, he being too far from the house to come home to his meals, and the farmer's wife so far carried out her intention of destroying him, that she poisoned his dinner. It was somewhat late in arriving, and the future prophet feeling exhausted from his honest exertions in his master's interest and from want of food, lay down on the heath and fell into a heavy slumber. In this position he was suddenly awakened by feeling somewhat cold in his breast, which on examination he found to be a small white stone, with a hole through the centre. He looked through it, when a vision appeared to him which revealed the treachery and diabolical intention of his mistress. To test the truth of the vision, he gave the dinner intended for himself to his faithful collie ; the poor brute writhed, and died soon after in the greatest agony.

The following version is supplied by Mr. Macintyre, teacher, Arpafeelie :—Although the various accounts as to the manner in which Coinneach Odhar became gifted with second-sight differ in some respects, yet they generally agree in this, that it was acquired while he was engaged in the humble occupation of cutting peats or divots, which were in his day, and still are in many places, used as fuel through-out the Highlands of Scotland. On the occasion referred to, being somewhat fatigued, he lay down, resting his head upon a little knoll, and waited the arrival of his wife with his dinner, whereupon he fell fast asleep. On awaking, he felt something hard under his head, and examining the cause of the uneasiness, discovered a small round stone with a hole through the middle. He picked it up, and looking through it, saw by the aid of this prophetic stone that his wife was coming to him with a dinner consisting of sowans and milk, polluted, though unknown to her, in a manner which, as well as several other particulars connected with it, we forbear to mention. But Coinneach found that though this stone was the means by which a supernatural power had been conferred upon him, it had, on its very first application, deprived him of the sight of that eye with which he looked through it, and he continued ever afterwards *cam*, or blind of an eye.

It would appear from this account that the intended murderer made use of the Seer's wife to convey the poison to her own husband, thus adding to her diabolical and murderous intention, by making her who would feel the loss the keenest, the medium by which her husband was to lose his life.

Hugh Miller, in his " Scenes and Legends in the North of Scotland," says :—When serving as a field labourer with a wealthy clansman who resided somewhere near Brahan Castle, he made himself so formidable to the clansman's wife by his shrewd, sarcastic humour, that she resolved on destroying him by poison. With this design, she mixed a preparation of noxious herbs with his food, when he was one day employed in digging turf in a solitary morass, and brought it to him in a pitcher. She found him lying asleep on one of those conical fairy hillocks which abound in some parts of the Highlands, and her courage failing her, instead of awaking him, she set down the pitcher by his side and returned home. He woke shortly after, and, seeing the food, would have begun his repast, but feeling something press heavily against his heart, he opened his waistcoat and found a beautiful smooth stone, resembling a pearl, but much larger, which had apparently been dropped into his breast while he slept. He gazed at it in admiration, and became conscious as he gazed, that a strange faculty of seeing the future as distinctly as the present, and men's real designs and motives as clearly as their actions, was miraculously imparted to him ; and it is well for him that he should become so knowing at such a crisis, for the first secret he became acquainted with was that of the treachery practised against him by his mistress.

We have thus several accounts of the manner in which our prophet obtained possession of his remarkable stone, white or blue, with or without a hole through its centre, it matters little ; that he did obtain it, we must assume to be beyond question ; but it is a matter for consideration, and indeed open to considerable doubt, whether it had any real prophetic virtue.   If Kenneth was really possessed of the power of prophecy he more than likely used the stone simply to impose upon the people, who would never believe him possessed of such a gift, unless they saw with their own eyes the means by which he exercised it.

We shall, as far as possible, give the Prophecies under the following headings—Those which might be attributed to great penetration and natural shrewdness ; those which are still unfulfilled ; those that are doubtful ; and those which have been unquestionably fulfilled, or partly fulfilled.

PROPHECIES WHICH MIGHT BE ATTRIBUTED

TO NATURAL SHREWDNESS.

HE no doubt predicted many things which the unbeliever in his prophetic gifts may ascribe to great natural shrewdness. Among these may be placed his prophecy, 150 years before the Caledonian Canal was built, that ships would some day sail round the back of Tomnahurich Hill. A gentleman in Inverness sent for Coinneach to take down his prophecies. He wrote several of them, but when he heard this one, he thought it so utterly absurd and impossible, that he threw the manuscript of what he had already written into the fire, and gave up any further communication with the Seer. Mr. Maclennan gives the following version of it :—" Strange as it may seem to you this day, time will come, and it is not far off, when full-rigged ships will be seen sailing eastward and westward by the back of Tomnahurich, near Inverness." Mr. Macintyre supplies us with a version in the Seer's vernacular Gaelic :—" Thig an latha 's am faicear laraichean Sasunnach air an tarruing le srianan corcaich seachad air cul Tom-na-hiuraich." (The day will come when English mares, with hempen bridles, shall be led round the back of Tomnahurich). It is quite possible that a man of penetration and great natural shrewdness might, from the appearance of the country, with its chain of great inland lakes, predict the future Caledonian Canal. Among others which might safely be predicted, without the aid of any supernatural gift, are " that the day will come when there will be a road through the hills of Ross-shire from sea to sea, and a bridge upon every stream." "That the people will degenerate as their country improves."   " That the clans will become so effeminate as to flee from their native country before an army of sheep." Mr. Macintyre supplies the following version of the latter : —Alluding possibly to the depopulation of the Highlands, Coinneach said " that the day will come when the Big Sheep will overrun the country until they strike (meet) the northern sea."   Big sheep here is commonly understood to mean deer, but whether the words signify sheep or deer, the prophecy has been very strikingly fulfilled.   The other two have also been only too literally fulfilled.

Mr. Macintyre supplies another version, as follows : " The day will come when the hills of Ross will be strewed with ribbons."   It is generally accepted that this prediction finds its fulfilment in the many good roads that now intersect the various districts of the country.   Other versions are given, such as ' a ribbon on every hill, and a bridge on every stream' (Raoban air gach cnoc agus drochaid air gach alltan) ; ' a mill on every river and a white house on every hillock ' (Muillinn air gach abhainn agus tigh geal air gach cnocan) ; and ' that the hills of the country will be crossed with shoulder-halts ' (criosan guaille).   Since Kenneth's day mills were very common, and among the most useful industrial institutions of the country, as may be evidenced by the fact that, even to this day, the proprietors of lands, where such establishments were once located, pay Crown and Bishop's rents for them.   And may we not discover the fulfilment of " a white house on every hillock " in the many elegant shooting lodges, hotels, and school-houses now found in every corner of the Highlands.

Mr. Maclennan supplies the following:—There is opposite the shore at Findon, Ferrintosh, two sand banks which were, in the time of the Seer, entirely covered over with the sea, even at the very lowest spring ebbs. Regarding these, Coinneach said, " that the day will come, however distant, when these banks will form the coast line ; and when that happens, know for a certainty that troublesome times are at hand." " These banks," our correspondent continues, " have been visibly approaching, for many years back, nearer and nearer to the shore." This is another of the class of predictions which might be attributed to natural shrewdness. It is being gradually fulfilled, and it may be well to watch for the " troublesome times," and so test the powers of the Seer.

Other predictions of this class may occur as we proceed, but we have no hesitation in saying that, however much natural penetration and shrewdness might have aided Kenneth in predicting such as these, it would assist him little in prophesying " that the day will come when Tomnahurich," or, as he called it, Tom-na-sithichean, or the Fairy Hill, " will be under lock and key, and the Fairies secured within." It would hardly assist him in foreseeing the beautiful and unique cemetery on the top of the hill, and the spirits (of the dead) chained within, as we now see it.

Since the last edition of the " Prophecies " appeared, our attention has been called to the following paragraph published in the *Inverness Advertiser*, in 1859 ; that is *before* it had been turned into a Cemetery—" Tomnahurich, the far-famed Fairies' Hill, has been sown with oats. According to tradition, the Brahan prophet who lived 200 years ago, predicted that ships with unfurled sails would pass and repass Tomnahurich ; and further, that it would yet be placed under lock and key. The first part of the prediction was verified by the opening of the Caledonian Canal, and we seem to be on the eve of seeing the realization of the rest by the final closing up of the Fairies' Hill." This paragraph was in print before the prediction was fulfilled.

UNFULFILLED PROPHECIES.

KENNETH foretold "that, however unlikely it may now appear, the Island of Lews will be laid waste by a destructive war, which will continue till the contending armies, slaughtering each other as they proceed, shall reach Tarbert in Harris. In the Caws of Tarbert, the retreating host will suddenly halt; an onslaught, led by a left-handed Macleod, called Donald, son of Donald, son of Donald, will then be made upon the pursuers. The only weapon in this champion's hands will be a black sooty *cabar*, taken off a neighbouring hut; but his intrepidity and courage will so inspirit the fugitives that they will fight like mighty men, and overpower their pursuers. The Lews will then enjoy a long period of repose." It has not hitherto been suggested that this prophecy has been fulfilled, and we here stake the reputation of our prophet upon its fulfilment, and that of the following predictions, which are still current throughout the Northern Counties of Scotland.

Another, by which the faith of future generations may be tested, is the one in which he predicted " that a Loch above Beauly will burst through its banks and destroy in its rush a village in its vicinity." We are not aware that such a calamity as is here foretold has yet occurred, nor are we aware of the locality of the loch or the village.

We have received various versions of the, as yet, unfulfilled prediction regarding " Clach an t-Seasaidh," near the

Muir of Ord. This is an angular stone, sharp at the top, which at one time stood upright, and was of considerable height. It is now partly broken and lying on the ground. " The day will come when the ravens will, from the top of it, drink their three fulls, for three successive days, of the blood of the Mackenzies."

Mr. Maclennan's version is :—" The day will come when the ravens will drink their full of the Mackenzies' blood three times off the top of the ' Clach Mhor,' and glad am I (continues the Seer) that I will not live to see that day, for a bloody and destructive battle will be fought on the Muir of Ord. A squint-eyed (cam), pox-pitted tailor will originate the battle ; for men will become so scarce in those days that each of seven women will strive hard for the squint-eyed tailor's heart and hand, and out of this strife the conflict will originate."

Mr. Macintyre writes regarding these :—" The prophecies that 'the raven will drink from the top of ' Clach an t-Seasaidh,' its full of the blood of the Mackenzies for three successive days,' and ' that the Mackenzies would be so reduced in numbers, that they would be all taken in an open fishing boat (scuta dubh) back to Ireland from whence they originally came,' remain still unfulfilled."

In the Kintail versions of these predictions they are made to apply to the Macraes, who are to get so scarce that a cripple tailor of the name is to be in such request among the ladies as to cause a desperate battle in the district between themselves and the Maclennans, the result of which will be that a black fishing wherry or " scuta dubh " will carry back to Ireland all that remains of the clan Macrae, but no sooner do they arrive than they again return to Kintail. Before this was to take place, nine men of the name of Macmillan would arrive at manhood (assume their bonnets) in the district; assemble at a funeral at Cnoc-a-Chlachain in Kilduich, and originate a quarrel. At this exact period, the Macraes would be at the height of their prosperity in Kintail, and henceforth begin to lose their hold in the country of their ancestors. The Macmillans have actually met in this spot and originated a quarrel as predicted, although nothing could have been more unlikely, for in the Seer's day there was not a single one of the name in Kintail, nor for several generations after. It is somewhat remarkable to find that the Maclennans are at this very time actually supplanting the Macraes as foretold, for the last two of the ancient stock—the late tenants of Fernaig and Leachachan—who left the district have been succeeded in their holdings by Maclennans; and other instances of the same kind, within recent years, are well known.

At present, we are happy to say, there does not appear much probability of the Clan Mackenzie being reduced to such small dimensions as would justify us in expecting the fulfilment of the " scuta dubh " part of the prophecy on a very early date. If the prediction, however, be confined in its application to the Mackenzies of Seaforth, it may be said to have been already almost fulfilled. We have, indeed, been told that this is a fragment of the unfulfilled prophecy uttered by Coinneach regarding the ultimate doom and total extinction of the Seaforths, and which we have been as yet unable to procure in detail. It was, however, known to Bernard Burke, who makes the following reference to it :—
" He (the Seer) uttered it in all its horrible length ; but I at present suppress the last portion of it, which is as yet unfulfilled. Every other part of the prediction has most literally and most accurately come to pass, but let us earnestly hope that the course of future events may at length give the lie to the avenging curse of the Seer. The

last clause of the prophecy is well-known to many of those versed in Highland family tradition, and I trust that it may remain unfulfilled."

One of our correspondents presumes that the mention of " Clach an t-Seasaidh " refers to the remains of a Druidical circle to be seen still on the right and left of the turnpike road at Windhill, near Beauly.   As a sign whereby to know when the latter prophecy would be accomplished, Coinneach said " that a mountain-ash tree will grow out of the walls of Fairburn Tower, and when it becomes large enough to form a cart axle, these things will come to pass."   Not long ago, a party informed us that a mountain-ash, or rowan-tree, was actually growing out of the tower walls, and was about the thickness of a man's thumb.

Various other unfulfilled predictions of the Seer remain to be noticed.   One is regarding "Clach an Tiompain," a well-known stone in the immediate vicinity of the far-famed Strathpeffer Wells.   It is, like " Clach-an-t-Seasaidh," an upright, pillar-looking stone, which, when struck, makes a great hollow sound or echo, and hence its designation, the literal meaning of which is the " stone of the hollow sound or echo."   Coinneach said " that the day will come when ships will ride with their cables attached to ' Clach-an-Tiompain."   It is perhaps superfluous to point out that this has not yet come to pass ; and we could only imagine two ways in which it was possible to happen, either by a canal being made through the valley of Strathpeffer, passing in the neighbourhood of the Clach, or by the removal of the stone some day by the authorities of " Baile Chail " to Dingwall pier.   They may feel disposed to thus aid the great prophet of their country to secure the position as a great man, which we now claim in his behalf.

While the first edition was going through the press we

visited Knockfarrel, in the immediate vicinity of Loch Ussie.
and we were told of another way in which this prediction
might be fulfilled so peculiar that, although it is altogether
improbable, nay impossible, that it can ever take place, we
shall reproduce it.   Having found our way to the top of this
magnificent and perfect specimen of a vitrified fort, we were
so struck with its great size, that we carefully paced it, and
found it to be one hundred and fifty paces in length, with a
uniform width of forty, both ends terminating in a semi-
circle, from each of which projected for a distance of sixty
paces, vitrified matter, as if it were originally a kind of
promenade, thus making the whole length of the structure
two hundred and seventy yards, or thereabout.   On the summit of the hill we met two boys herding cows, and as our
previous experience taught us that boys, as a rule—especially herd boys—are acquainted with the traditions and
places of interest in the localities they frequent, we were
curious enough to ask them if they ever heard of Coinneach Odhar in the district, and if he ever said anything
regarding the fort on Knockfarrel.   They directed us to
what they called " Fingal's Well," in the interior of the
ruined fort, and informed us that this well was used by the
inhabitants of the fortress "until Fingal, one day, drove
them out, and placed a large stone over the well, which has
ever since kept the water from oozing up, after which he
jumped to the other side of the (Strathpeffer) valley."
There being considerable rains for some days previous to
our visit, water could be seen in the "well."   One of the
boys drove down a stick until it struck the stone, producing
a hollow sound which unmistakably indicated the existence
of a cavity beneath.   "Coinneach Odhar foretold," said
the boy, " that if ever that stone was taken out of its place,
Loch Ussie would ooze up through the well and flood the

valley below to such an extent that ships could sail up to
Strathpeffer and be fastened to ' Clach-an-Tiompain' ; and
this would happen after the stone had fallen three times.   It
has already fallen twice," continued our youthful informant,
"and you can now see it newly raised, strongly and carefully
propped up, near the end of the doctor's house."   And so it
is, and can still be seen, on the right, a few paces from the
roadside, as you proceed up to the Strathpeffer Wells.   We
think it right to give this—a third—with the other versions,
for probably the reader will admit that the one is just as
likely to happen as the other.   We can quite understand
Kenneth prophesying that the sea would yet reach Strathpeffer ; for to any one standing where we did, on the summit
of Knockfarrel, the bottom of the valley appears much lower
than the Cromarty Firth beyond Dingwall, and it looks as
if it might, any day, break through the apparently slender
natural embankment below Tulloch Castle, which seemed,
from where we stood, to be the only obstruction in its path.
We need, however, hardly inform the reader in the district
that the bottom of the Strathpeffer valley is, in reality,
several feet above the present sea level.

Another prediction is that concerning the Canonry of
Ross, which is still standing—" The day will come when,
full of the Mackenzies, it will fall with a fearful crash."
This may come to pass in several ways.   The Canonry is
the principal burying-place of the Clan, and it may fall
when full of dead Mackenzies, or when a large concourse
of the Clan is present at the funeral of a great chief.

" When two false teachers shall come across the seas who
will revolutionize the religion of the land, and nine bridges
shall span the river Ness, the Highlands will be overrun by
ministers without grace and women without shame," is a
prediction which some maintain has all the appearance of

being rapidly fulfilled at this moment.   It has been suggested that the two false teachers were no other than the great evangelists, Messrs. Moody and Sankey, who, no doubt, from Coinneach Odhar's standpoint of orthodoxy, who must have been a Roman Catholic or an Episcopalian, attempted to revolutionize the religion of the Highlands. If this be so, the other portions of the prophecy are looming not far off in the immediate future.   We have already eight bridges on the Ness—the eighth has only been completed last year—and the ninth is almost finished.   If we are to accept the opinions of certain of the clergy themselves, " ministers without grace " are becoming the rule, and as for a plenitude of " women without shame," ask any ancient matron, and she will at once tell you that Kenneth's prophecy may be held to have been fulfilled in that particular any time within the last half century.   Gleidh sinne ! !

It is possible the following may have something to do with the same calamity in the Highlands.   Mr. Maclennan says : —With reference to some great revolution which shall take place in the country, Coinneach Odhar said that " before that event shall happen, the water of the river Beauly will thrice cease to run.   On one of these occasions a salmon, having shells instead of scales, will be found in the bed of the river."   This prophecy has been in part fulfilled, for the Beauly has on two occasions ceased to run, and a salmon of the kind mentioned has been found in the bed of the river.

Mr. Macintyre gives another version :—" When the river Beauly is dried up three times, and a ' scaly salmon ' or royal sturgeon, is caught in the river, that will be a time of great trial."   (Nuair a thraoghas abhainn na Manachain tri uairean, agus a ghlacair Bradan Sligeach air grunnd na h-aibhne, 's ann an sin a bhitheas an deuchainn ghoirt.) The river has been already dried up twice, the last time in

1826, and a ' Bradan Sligeach,' or royal sturgeon, measuring nine feet in length, has been caught in the estuary of the Beauly about two years ago.

The following is one which we trust may never be realized in all its details, though some may be disposed to think that signs are not wanting of its ultimate fulfilment :—" The day will come when the jaw-bone of the big sheep, or " caoirich mhora,' will put the plough on the rafters (air an aradh) ; when sheep shall become so numerous that the bleating of the one shall be heard by the other from Conchra in Loch-alsh to Bun-da-Loch in Kintail they shall be at their height in price, and henceforth will go back and deteriorate, until they disappear altogether, and be so thoroughly forgotten that a man finding the jaw-bone of a sheep in a cairn, will not recognise it, or be able to tell what animal it belonged to.   The ancient proprietors of the soil shall give place to strange merchant proprietors, and the whole Highlands will become one huge deer forest ; the whole country will be so utterly desolated and depopulated that the crow of a cock shall not be heard north of Druim-Uachdair ; the people will emigrate to Islands now unknown, but which shall yet be discovered in the boundless oceans, after which the deer and other wild animals in the huge wilderness shall be exterminated and drowned by horrid *black* rains (siantan dubha).   The people will then return and take undisturbed possession of the lands of their ancestors."

We have yet to see the realization of the following :—" A dun, hornless, cow (supposed to mean a steamer) will appear in the Minch (off Carr Point, in Gairloch), and make a ' geum,' or bellow, which will knock the six chimneys off Gairloch House." (Thig bo mhaol odhar a steach an t-Aite-mor agus leigeas i geum aiste 'chuireas na se beannagan dheth an Tigh Dhige).   Gairloch House, or the Tigh Dige of Coinneach's day, was the old house which stood in the park on the right, as you proceed from the bridge in the direction of the present mansion. The walls were of wattled twigs, wicker work, or plaited twig hurdles, thatched with turf or divots, and surrounded with a deep ditch, which could, in time of approaching danger, be filled with water from the river, hence the name " Tigh Dige," House of the Ditch. It has been suggested that the Seer's prediction referred to this stronghold, but a strong objection to this view appears in the circumstance that the ancient citadel had no chimneys to fall off. The present mansion is, however, also called the " Tigh Dige," and it has the exact number of chimneys—six.

" The day will come when a river in Wester Ross shall be dried up." " The day will come when there shall be such dire persecution and bloodshed in the county of Sutherland, that people can ford the river Oykel dryshod, over dead men's bodies." " The day will come when a raven, attired in plaid and bonnet, will drink his full of human blood on ' Fionn-bheinn,' three times a day, for three successive days."

" A battle will be fought at Ault-nan-Torcan, in the Lewis, which will be a bloody one indeed. It will truly take place, though the time may be far hence, but woe to the mothers of sucklings that day. The defeated host will continue to be cut down till it reaches Ard-a-chaolais (a place nearly seven miles from Ault-nan-Torcan), and there the swords will make terrible havoc." This has not yet occurred.

Speaking of what should come to pass in the parish of Lochs, he said—" At bleak Runish in Lochs, they will spoil and devour, at the foot of the crags, and will split heads by the score." He is also said to have predicted " that the day will come when the raven will drink its three fulls of the blood of the Clan Macdonald on the top of the Hills of Minaraidh in Parks, in the parish of Lochs." This looks as if the one above predicted about the Mackenzies had been misapplied to the Macdonalds. "The day will come when there shall be a laird of Tulloch who will kill four wives in succession, but the fifth shall kill him."

Regarding the battle of Ard-nan-Ceann, at Benbecula, North Uist, he said—"Oh, Ard-nan-Ceann, Ard-nan-Ceann, glad am I that I will not be at the end of the South Clachan that day, when the young men will be weary and faint; for Ard-nan-Ceann will be the scene of a terrible conflict."

"A severe battle will be fought at the (present) Ardelve market stance, in Lochalsh, when the slaughter will be so great that people can cross the ferry over dead men's bodies. The battle will be finally decided by a powerful man and his five sons, who will come across from the Strath (the Achamore district)."

Coinneach said—"When a holly bush (or tree) shall grow out of the face of the rock at Torr-a-Chuilinn (Kintail) to a size sufficiently large to make a shaft for a 'carn-slaoid' (sledge-cart), a battle will be fought in the locality."

"When Loch Shiel, in Kintail, shall become so narrow that a man can leap across it, the salmon shall desert the Loch and the River Shiel." We are told that the Loch is rapidly getting narrower at a particular point, by the action of the water on the banks and bottom, and that if it goes on as it has done in recent years it can easily be leaped at no distant date. Prudence would suggest a short lease of these Salmon Fishings.

He also predicted that a large stone, standing on the hill opposite Scallisaig farm-house, in Glenelg, "will fall and kill a man." This boulder is well-known to people in the district, and the prophecy is of such a definite character, that there cannot possibly be any mistake about its meaning or its fulfilment should such a calamity ever unfortunately take place.

PROPHECIES AS TO THE FULFILMENT OF
WHICH THERE IS A DOUBT.

WHEN a magpie (pitheid) shall have made a nest for three successive years in the gable of the Church of Ferrintosh, the church will fall when full of people," is one of those regarding which we find it difficult to decide whether it has been already fulfilled or not. Mr. Macintyre, who supplies this version, adds the following remarks :—The Church of Ferrintosh was known at an earlier period as the Parish Church of Urquhart and Loggie. Some maintain that this prediction refers to the Church of Urray. Whether this be so or not, there were circumstances connected with the Church of Ferrintosh in the time of the famous Rev. Dr. Macdonald, which seemed to indicate the beginning of the fulfilment of the prophecy, and which led to very alarming consequences. A magpie actually did make her nest in the church gable, exactly as foretold. This, together with a rent between the church wall and the stone stairs which led up to the gallery, seemed to favour the opinion that the prophecy was on the eve of being accomplished, and people felt uneasy when they glanced upon the ominous nest, the rent in the wall, and the crowded congregation, and remembered Coinneach's prophecy, as they walked into the church to hear the Doctor. It so happened one day that the church was unusually full of people, insomuch that it was found necessary to connect the ends of the seats with planks, in order

to accommodate them all.   Unfortunately, one of those
temporary seats was either too weak, or too heavily burdened : it snapped in two with a loud report and startled
the audience.   Coinneach Odhar's prophecy flashed across
their minds, and a simultaneous rush was made by the
panic-stricken congregation to the door.   Many fell, and
were trampled underfoot, while others fainted, being
seriously crushed and bruised.

Among a rural population, sayings and doings, applicable
to a particular parish, crop up, and, in after times, are
applied to occurrences in neighbouring parishes.   Having
regard to this may it not be suggested that, what is current
locally in regard to Ferrintosh and Coinneach's sayings, may
only be a transcript of an event now matter of history in a
parish on the northern side of the Cromarty Firth.   We
refer to the destruction of the Abbey Church at Fearn by
lightning, October 10, 1742.   We have never seen a de-
tailed account of this sad accident in print, and have no
doubt the reader will be glad to have a graphic description of
it from the pen of Bishop Forbes, the famous author of the
" Jacobite Memoirs," who visited his diocese of Ross and
Caithness in the summer of 1762.   This account is taken
from his unpublished MS. Journal, now the property of the
College of Bishops of the Scottish Episcopal Church, and
presently in the hands of the Rev. F. Smith, Arpafeelie, who
has kindly permitted us to make the following extract :—

" The ruinous Church of Ferne was of old an Abbacy of
White Friars (see Keith's Catalogue, p. 247).   The roof of
flagstones, with part of a side wall, was beat down in an
instant by thunder and lightning on Sunday, October 10th,
1742, and so crushed and bruised forty persons, that they
were scarcely to be discovered, who or what they were, and
therefore, were buried promiscuously, without any manner

of distinction. The gentry, having luckily their seats in the niches, were saved from the sudden crash, as was the preacher by the sounding-boards falling upon the pulpit and his bowing down under it. Great numbers were wounded (see Scot's Magazine for 1742, p. 485). But there is a most material circumstance not mentioned, which has been carefully concealed from the publishers, and it is this : By a Providential event, this was the first Sunday that the Rev. and often-mentioned Mr. Stewart, had a congregation near Cadboll, in view of Ferne, whereby many lives were saved, as the kirk was far from being so throng as usual, and that he and his people, upon coming out from worship, and seeing the dismal falling-in just when it happened, hastened with all speed to the afflictive spot, and dragged many of the wounded out of the rubbish, whose cries would have pierced a heart of adamant. Had not this been the happy case, I speak within bounds when I say two, if not three, to one, would have perished. Some of the wounded died. This church has been a large and lofty building, as the walls are very high, and still standing."

It has been suggested that the prediction was fulfilled by the falling to pieces of the Church at the Disruption ; but we would be loth to stake the reputation of our prophet on this assumption.

Another, supposed by some to be fulfilled by the annual visits of the militia for their annual drill, is—" That when a wood on the Muir of Ord grows to a man's height, regiments of soldiers shall be seen there drawn up in battle order."

In connection with the battle, or battles, at Cille-Chriosd and the Muir of Ord, Mr. Macintyre says :—The Seer foretold that " Fear Ruadh an Uird (the Red Laird of Ord) would be carried home, wounded, on blankets." Whether this saying has reference to an event looming in the distant future, or is a fragment of a tradition regarding sanguinary events well known in the history of Cille-Chriosd, and of which a full and graphic account, both in prose and verse, can be seen on pp. 82-86 and 136-139, Vol. I. of the *Celtic Magazine*, it is impossible to say.

PROPHECIES WHOLLY OR PARTLY FULFILLED.

HERE are several additional predictions which have been wholly or partly fulfilled. " The day will come when the Mackenzies will lose all their possessions in Lochalsh, after which it will fall into the hands of an Englishman, who shall be distinguished by great liberality to his people, and lavish expenditure of money. He will have one son and two daughters; and, after his death, the property will revert to the Mathesons, its original possessors, who will build a Castle on Druim-a-Dubh, at Balmacarra." The late Mr. Lillingstone was an Englishman. He was truly distinguished for kindness and liberality to his tenants, and he had a son and two daughters, although, we are informed, he had been married for seventeen years before he had any family. When he came into possession, old people thought they discerned the fulfilment of a part of Kenneth's prediction in his person, until it was remarked that he had no family as foretold by the Seer. At last, a son and two daughters were successively born to Mr. Lillingstone. After his death, the son sold the whole of Lochalsh to Alexander Matheson, M.P. for the Counties of Ross and Cromarty, and, so far, the prediction has been realized. A castle has been built at Duncraig, a considerable distance from the spot predicted by the Seer; but if Kenneth is to be depended upon, a castle will yet be built by one of the Mathesons on Druim-a-Dubh, at Balmacarra. Had this prophecy been got up after the event, the reputation of the Seer would certainly not have been staked on the erection of another castle in the remote future, when the Mathesons already possess such a magnificent mansion at Duncraig.

During a recent visit to the Island of Raasay we received a peculiar prediction regarding the Macleods from an old man there, over eighty years of age, who remembered seven proprietors of Raasay, and who sorely lamented the fulfilment of the prophecy, and the decline of the good old stock, entirely in consequence of their own folly and extravagance. Since then, we had the prediction repeated by a Kintail man in identical terms ; and as it is hardly translatable, we shall give it in the original vernacular :—" Dar a thig Mac-Dhomhnuill Duibh bàn ; MacShimidh ceann-dearg ; Sisealach claon ruadh ; Mac-Coinnich mor bodhar ; agus Mac-Gille-challum cama-chasach, iar-ogha Ian bhig à Ruiga, se' sin a Mac-Gille-challum is miosa 'thainig na thig ; cha bhi mi ann ri linn, 's cha'n fhearr leam air a bhith." (When we shall have a fair-haired Lochiel ; a red-haired Lovat ; a squint-eyed, fair-haired Chisholm ; a big deaf Mackenzie ; and a bow-crooked-legged MacGille-challum, who shall be the great-grand-son of John Beg, or little John, of Ruiga : that Mac-Gille-challum will be the worst that ever came or ever will come ; I shall not be in existence in his day, and I have no desire that I should). Ruiga is the name of a place in Skye. When the last Macleod of Raasay was born, an old sage in the district called upon his neighbour, and told him, with an expression of great sorrow, that Mac-Gille-challum of Raasay now had an heir, and his birth was a certain forerunner of the extinction of his house. Such an event as the birth of an heir had been hitherto, in this as in all other Highland families, universally considered an occasion for great rejoicing among

D

the retainers. The other old man was amazed, and asked the sage what he meant by such unusual and disloyal remarks. "Oh!" answered he, "do you not know that this is the grand-grandson of John Beg of Ruiga whom Coinneach Odhar predicted would be the worst of his race." And so he undoubtedly proved himself to be, for he lost for ever the ancient inheritance of his house, and acted generally in such a manner as to fully justify the Seer's prediction; and what is still more remarkable, the Highland lairds, with the peculiar characteristics and malformations foretold by Kenneth, preceded or were the contemporaries of the last MacGille-challum of Raasay.

Here is a prediction of the downfall of another distinguished Highland family—Clan Ranald of the Isles. "The day will come when the old wife with the footless stocking (cailleach nam mogan) will drive the Lady of Clan Ranald from Nunton House, in Benbecula." We are informed that this was fulfilled when the Macdonalds took the farm of Nunton, locally known as "Baile na Caillich." Old Mrs. Macdonald was in the habit of wearing these primitive articles of dress, and was generally known in the district as "Cailleach nam Mogan." Clan Ranald and his lady, like many more of our Highland chiefs, ultimately went to the wall, and the descendants of the "old wife with the footless stocking" occupied, and, for anything we know, still occupy the ancient residence of the long-distinguished race of Clan Ranald of the Isles.

In the beginning of the seventeenth century, and during the Seer's lifetime, there lived in Kintail an old man— Duncan Macrae—who was curious to know by what means he should end his days. He applied to a local female Seer, who informed him that he "would die by the sword" (le bàs a chlaidheamh). This appeared so improbable in the case of such an old man, who had taken part in so many bloody frays and invariably escaped unhurt, that the matter was referred to the greater authority, Coinneach Odhar. He corroborated the woman, but still the matter was almost universally discredited in the district, and by none more so than by old Duncan himself. However, years after, conviction was forced upon them; for, according to the "Genealogy of the Macraes," written by the Rev. John Macrae, minister of Dingwall, who died in 1704—" Duncan being an old man in the year 1654, when General Monk, afterwards Duke of Albemarle, came to Kintail, retired from his house in Glenshiel to the hills, where, being found by some of the soldiers who had straggled from the body of the army in hopes of plunder, and who, speaking to him roughly, in a language he did not understand, he, like Old Orimanus, drew his sword, &c., and was immediately killed by them. This was all the blood that General Monk or his soldiers, amounting to 1500 men, had drawn, and all the opposition he met with, although the Earl of Middleton and Sir George Monro were within a few miles of them, and advertised of their coming, Seaforth having been sent by Middleton to the Isle of Skye and parts adjoining, to treat with the Macdonalds and the Macleods, &c."

Regarding the evictions which would take place in the Parish of Petty, he said, "The day will come, and it is not far off, when farm-steadings will be so few and far between, that the crow of a cock shall not be heard from the one steading to the other." This prediction has certainly been fulfilled, for, in the days of the Seer there were no fewer than sixteen tenants on the farm of Morayston alone.

On the south of the bay, at Petty, is an immense stone, of at least eight tons weight, which formerly marked the boundary between the estates of Culloden and Moray. On the

20th of February, 1799, it was mysteriously removed from its former position, and carried about 260 yards into the sea.   It is supposed by some that this was brought about by an earthquake ; others think that the stone was carried off by the action of ice, combined with the influence of a tremendous hurricane, which blew from the shore, during that fearful and stormy night.   It was currently reported, and pretty generally believed at the time, that his Satanic Majesty had a finger in this work.   Be that as it may, there is no doubt whatever that the Brahan Seer predicted " that the day will come when the Stone of Petty, large though it is, and high and dry upon the land as it appears to people this day, will be suddenly found as far advanced into the sea as it now lies away from it inland, and no one will see it removed, or be able to account for its sudden and marvellous transportation."

The Seer was at one time in the Culloden district on some important business.   While passing over what is now so well known as the Battlefield of Culloden, he exclaimed, "Oh ! Drummossie, thy bleak moor shall, ere many generations have passed away, be stained with the best blood of the Highlands.   Glad am I that I will not see that day, for it will be a fearful period ; heads will be lopped off by the score, and no mercy will be shown or quarter given on either side."   It is perhaps unnecessary to point out how literally this prophecy has been fulfilled on the occasion of the last battle fought on British soil.   We have received several other versions of it from different parts of the country almost all in identical terms.

" The time will come when whisky or dram shops will be so plentiful that one may be met with almost at the head of every plough furrow."   (Thig an latha 's am bi tighean-oil cho lionmhor 's nach mor nach fhaicear tigh-osda aig ceann gach claise.) " Policemen will become so numerous in every town that they may be met with at the corner of every street." " Travelling merchants " [pedlars and hawkers] " will be so plentiful that a person can scarcely walk a mile on the public highway without meeting one of them."

The following is from " A Summer in Skye," by the late Alex. Smith, author of " A Life Drama." Describing Dunvegan Castle and its surroundings, he says :—" Dun Kenneth's prophecy has come to pass—' In the days of Norman, son of the third Norman, there will be a noise in the doors of the people, and wailing in the house of the widow ; and Macleod will not have so many gentlemen of his name as will row a five-oared boat round the Maidens.' If the last trumpet had been sounded at the end of the French war, no one but a Macleod would have risen out of the churchyard of Dunvegan. If you want to see a chief (of the Macleods) now-a-days you must go to London for him." There can be no question as to these having been fulfilled to the letter.

" The day will come when a fox will rear a litter of cubs on the hearthstone of Castle Downie." " The day will come when a fox, white as snow, will be killed on the west coast of Sutherlandshire." " The day will come when a wild deer will be caught alive at Chanonry Point, in the Black Isle." All these things have come to pass.

With respect to the clearances in Lewis, he said— " Many a long waste feannag (rig, once arable) will yet be seen between Uig of the Mountains and Ness of the Plains." That this prediction has been fulfilled to the letter, no one acquainted with the country will deny.

The following would appear to have been made solely on account of the unlikelihood of the occurrence :—" A Lochalsh woman shall weep over the grave of a Frenchman in the burying-place of Lochalsh." People imagined they

could discern in this an allusion to some battle on the West
Coast, in which French troops would be engaged ; but there
was an occurrence which gave it a very different interpre-
tation.   A native of Lochalsh married a French footman,
who died, shortly after this event, and was interred in the
burying-ground of Lochalsh, thus leaving his widow to
mourn over his grave.   This may appear a commonplace
matter enough, but it must be remembered that a Frenchman in Lochalsh, and especially a Frenchman whom a
Highland woman would mourn over, in Coinneach's day,
was a very different phenomenon to what it is in our days
of railways, tourists and steamboats.

The Seer also predicted the formation of a railway
through the Muir of Ord, handed down in the following
stanza :—

> Nuair a bhios da eaglais an Sgire na Toiseachd,
> A's lamh da ordaig an I-Stian,'
> Da dhrochaid aig Sguideal nan geocaire,
> As fear da imleag an Dunean,
> Thig Miltearan a Carn a-chlarsair,
> Air Carbad gun each gun srian,
> A dh-fhagas am Blar-dubh na fhasach,
> 'Dortadh fuil le iomadh sgian ;
> A's olaidh am fitheach a thri saitheachd
> De dh-fhuil nan Gaidheal, bho clach nam Fionn.

Here is a literal translation :—

> When there shall be two churches in the Parish of Ferrintosh,
> And a hand with two thumbs in " I-Stiana,"
> Two bridges at " Sguideal " (Conon) of the gormandizers,
> And a man with two navels at Dunean,
> Soldiers will come from " Carr a Chlarsair " (Tarradale)
> On a chariot without horse or bridle,
> Which will leave the " Blar-dubh " (Muir of Ord) a wilderness,
> Spilling blood with many knives ;
> And the raven shall drink his three fulls
> Of the blood of the Gael from the Stone of Fionn.

We already have two churches in the Parish of Ferrintosh, two bridges at Conon, and we are told by an eye-witness, that there is actually at this very time a man with two thumbs on each hand in " I-Stiana," in the Black Isle, and a man in the neighbourhood of Dunean who has two navels. The " chariot without horse or bridle " is undoubtedly the " iron horse." What particular event the latter part of the prediction refers to, it is impossible to say ; but if we are to have any faith in the Seer, something serious is looming not very remotely in the future.

Mr. Macintyre supplies the following, which is clearly a fragment of the one above given :—Coinneach Odhar fore-saw the formation of a railway through the Muir of Ord which he said " would be a sign of calamitous times." The prophecy regarding this is handed down to us in the follow-ing form :—" I would not like to live when a black bridleless horse shall pass through the Muir of Ord." " Fearchair a Ghunna " (Farquhar of the Gun, an idiotic simpleton who lived during the latter part of his extraordinary life on the Muir of Tarradale) seems, in his own quaint way, to have entered into the spirit of this prophecy, when he compared the train, as it first passed through the district, to the funeral of " Old Nick." Tradition gives another version, viz. :— " that after four successive dry summers, a fiery chariot shall pass through the ' Blar Dubh,' " which has been very literally fulfilled. Coinneach Odhar was not the only person that had a view beforehand of this railway line, for it is commonly reported that a man residing in the neighbour-hood of Beauly, gifted with second-sight, had a vision of the train moving along in all its headlong speed, when he was on his way home one dark autumn night, several years before the question of forming a railway in those parts was mooted.

Here are two other Gaelic stanzas having undoubted reference to the Mackenzies of Rosehaugh :—

Bheir Tanaistear Chlann Choinnich
Rocus *bàn* ás a choille ;
'S bheir e ceile bho tigh-ciuil
Le a mhuinntir 'na aghaidh ;
'S gum bi 'n Tanaistear mor
Ann an gniomh 's an ceann-labhairt,
'Nuair bhios am Pap' anns an Roimh
Air a thilgeadh dheth chaithair,

Thall fa chomhar Creag-a-Chodh
Comhnuichidh taillear caol odhar ;
'S Seumas gorach mar thighearn,
'S Seumas glic mar fhear tomhais—
A mharcaicheas gun srian
Air loth fhiadhaich a roghainn ;
Ach cuiridh mor-chuis gun chiall
'N aite siol nam fiadh siol nan gobhar ;
'S tuitidh an t-Eilean-dubh briagha
Fuidh riaghladh iasgairean Auch.

Literal translation :—

The heir (or chief) of the Mackenzies will take
A white rook out of the wood,
And will take a wife from a music house (dancing saloon),
With his people against him !
And the heir will be great
In deeds and as an orator,
When the Pope in Rome
Will be thrown off his throne.

Over opposite *Creag-a-Chow*
Will dwell a diminutive lean tailor,
Also Foolish James as the laird,
And Wise James as a measurer.
Who will ride without a bridle
The wild colt of his choice ;
But foolish pride without sense
Will put in the place of the seed of the deer the seed of the goat,
And the beautiful Black Isle will fall
Under the management of the fishermen of Avoch.

We have not learnt that any of the Rosehaugh Mackenzies has yet taken a *white* rook from the woods ; nor have we heard anything suggested as to what this part of the prophecy may refer to. We are, however, credibly informed that one of the late Mackenzies of Rosehaugh had taken his wife from a music saloon in one of our southern cities, and that his people were very much against him for so doing. One of them, Sir George, no doubt was " great in deeds and as an orator," but we fail to discover any connection between the time in which he lived and the time " when the Pope in Rome will be thrown off his throne." We were unable in the first edition to suggest the meaning of the first six lines of the last stanza, but Mr. Maclennan supplies us with the following explanation :—" I have been hearing these lines discussed since I was a boy, and being a native of Rosehaugh, I took a special interest in everything concerning it. The first two lines I was repeatedly informed, referred to a pious man who lived on the estate of Bennetsfield, opposite Craigiehow, when ' Seumas Gorach' (Foolish James referred to in the third line), was proprietor of Rosehaugh. This godly man, who was contemporary with Foolish James, often warned him of his end, and predicted his fate if he did not mend his ways ; and as he thus *cut* his bounds for him, he is supposed to be the ' diminutive lean tailor.' He is still in life. We all knew ' Foolish James.' The fourth line refers to James Maclaren, who lived at Rosehaugh most of the time during which the last two Mackenzies ruled over it, and only died two years ago. He was an odd character, but a very straightforward man ; often rebuked ' Foolish James ' for the reckless and fearless manner in which he rode about, and set bounds before the ' foolish laird,' which he was not allowed to pass. Maclaren was, on that account, believed to be the ' measurer' referred to by the Seer. The fifth and sixth lines are supposed to apply to the wife fancied by Mackenzie in a ' dancing saloon,' who was always considered the ' wild colt,' at whose instigation he rode so recklessly and foolishly." We wish the realizations of our prophet's predictions in this case were a little less fanciful.

Those in the seventh and eighth lines have been most literally fulfilled, for there can be no doubt that " foolish pride without sense " has brought about what the Seer predicted, and secured, for the present at least, the seed of the goat where the seed of the deer used to rule. The deer, and the deer's horns, as is well known, are the armorial bearings of the Mackenzies, while the goat is that of the Fletchers, who now rule in Rosehaugh, on the ruins of its once great and famous " Cabair-feidh."

Part of the beautiful Black Isle has already fallen under the management of the son of a fisherman of Avoch; and who knows but other fishermen from that humble village may yet amass sufficient wealth to buy the whole. The old proprietors, we regret, are rapidly making way with their " foolish pride without sense," for some one to purchase it.

We are informed that the present proprietor of Rosehaugh is the son of an Avoch fisherman—the son of a Mr. Jack, who followed that honourable avocation in this humble village for many years ; afterwards left the place and went to reside in Elgin, where he commenced business as a small general dealer, or " huckster ; " that some of the boys—his sons—exhibited a peculiar smartness while in school ; that this was noticed by a lady relative of their mother, an aunt, of the name of Fletcher, who encouraged and helped on the education of the boys, and who took one or more of them to her own home, and brought them up ; afterwards they found their way south, and ultimately became success-

ful merchants and landed proprietors.*   These are facts of
which we were entirely ignorant when first writing down the
stanzas already given.   The verses were sent to us from
various quarters, and they have undoubtedly been floating
about the country for generations.   So much for the Seer's
prophetic power in this instance.   Were we better
acquainted with the history of the other families referred to
in the stanzas, it is probable that more light could be thrown
upon what they refer to than we are at present able to do.

While we are dealing with the " wonderful " in connection with the House of Rosehaugh, it may not be out of
place to give a few instances of the somewhat extraordinary
experiences of the famous Sir George Mackenzie of Rosehaugh already referred to.   He was one of the most dis-
inguished members of the Scottish Bar, was Lord Advocate
for Scotland in the reign of Charles the Second, and was,
indeed, a contemporary of the Brahan Seer.   His " Insti-
tutes " are still considered a standing authority by the
legal profession :—On one occasion, while at Rosehaugh, a
poor widow from a neighbouring estate called to consult
him regarding her being repeatedly warned to remove from
a small croft which she held under a lease of several years ;
but as some time had yet to run before its expiry, and being
threatened with summary ejection from the croft, she went
to solicit his advice.   Having examined the tenor of the
lease, Sir George informed her that it contained a flaw,

*In corroboration of the main facts here stated we quote the following
from " Walford's County Families of the United Kingdom " :—
" FLETCHER, JAMES, Esq. of Rosehaugh, Ross-shire, son of the late Wm.
Jack, Esq., by Isabel, dau. of the late Charles Fletcher, Esq., and brother of
J. C. Fletcher, Esq. ; b 18— ; m 1852, Frederica Mary, dau. of John
Stephen, Esq., niece of Sir Alfred Stephen, C.B., Chief Justice of New
South Wales, and widow of Alexander Hay, Esq., of the 58th Regt. . . . .
He assumed the name of Fletcher in lieu of his patronymic on the death
of his mother in 1856."

which, in case of opposition, would render her success exceedingly doubtful ; and although it was certainly an oppressive act to deprive her of her croft, he thought her best plan was to submit. However, seeing the distressed state of mind in which the poor woman was on hearing his opinion, he desired her to call upon him the following day, when he would consider her case more carefully. His clerk, who always slept in the same room as his lordship, was not a little surprised, about midnight, to discover him rising from his bed fast asleep, lighting a candle which stood on his table, drawing in his chair, and commencing to write very busily, as if he had been all the time wide awake. The clerk saw how he was employed, but he never spoke a word, and, when he had finished, he saw him place what he had written in his private desk, locking it, extinguishing the candle, and then retiring to bed as if nothing had happened. Next morning at breakfast, Sir George remarked that he had had a very strange dream about the poor widow's threatened ejectment, which, he could now remember, and he had now no doubt of making out a clear case in her favour. His clerk rose from the table, asked for the key of his desk, and brought therefrom several pages of manuscript ; and, as he handed them to Sir George, enquired—" Is that like your dream ?" On looking over it for a few seconds, Sir George said, " Dear me, this is singular ; this is my very dream ! " He was no less surprised when his clerk informed him of the manner in which he had acted ; and, sending for the widow, he told her what steps to adopt to frustrate the efforts of her oppressors. Acting on the counsel thus given, the poor widow was ultimately successful, and, with her young family, was allowed to remain in possession of her " wee bit croftie " without molestation.

Sir George principally resided at this time in Edinburgh,

and, before dinner, invariably walked for half-an-hour. The place he selected for this was Leith Walk, then almost a solitary place. One day, while taking his accustomed exercise, he was met by a venerable-looking, grey-headed old gentleman, who accosted him, and, without introduction or apology, said—" There is a very important case to come off in London fourteen days hence, at which your presence will be required. It is a case of heirship to a very extensive estate in the neighbourhood of London, and a pretended claimant is doing his utmost to disinherit the real heir, on the ground of his inability to produce proper titles thereto. It is necessary that you be there on the day mentioned ; and in one of the attics of the mansion-house on the estate there is an old oak chest with two bottoms ; between these you will find the necessary titles, written on parchment." Having given this information, the old man disappeared, leaving Sir George quite bewildered ; but the latter, resuming his walk, soon recovered his previous equanimity, and thought nothing further of the matter.

Next day, while taking his walk in the same place, he was again met by the same old gentleman, who earnestly urged him not to delay another day in repairing to London, assuring him that he would be handsomely rewarded for his trouble ; but to this Sir George paid no particular attention. The third day he was again met by the same hoary-headed sire, who energetically pleaded with him not to lose a day in setting out, otherwise the case would be lost. His singular deportment, and his anxiety that Sir George should be present at the discussion of the case, in which he seemed so deeply interested, induced Sir George to give in to his earnest importunities, and accordingly he started next morning on horseback, arriving in London on the day preceding that on which the case was to come on. In a few hours he was pacing in front of the mansion-house described by the old man at Leith Walk, where he met two gentlemen engaged in earnest conversation—one of the claimants to the property, and a celebrated London barrister —to whom he immediately introduced himself as the principal law-officer of the crown for Scotland. The barrister, no doubt supposing that Sir George was coming to take the bread out of his mouth, addressed him in a surly manner, and spoke disrespectfully of his country ; to which the latter replied, " that, lame and ignorant as his learned friend took the Scotch to be, yet in law, as well as in other respects, they would effect what would defy him and all his London clique." This disagreeable dialogue was put an end to by the other gentleman—the claimant to the property—taking Sir George into the house. After sitting and conversing for some minutes, Sir George expressed a wish to be shown over the house. The drawing-room was hung all round with magnificent pictures and drawings, which Sir George greatly admired ; but there was one which particularly attracted his attention ; and after examining it very minutely he, with a surprised expression, inquired of his conductor whose picture it was ? and received answer—" It is my great-great-grandfather's." " My goodness ! " exclaimed Sir George, " the very man who spoke to me three times on three successive days in Leith Walk, and at whose urgent request I came here ! " Sir George, at his own request, was then conducted to the attics, in one of which there was a large mass of old papers, which was turned up and examined without discovering anything to assist them in prosecuting the claim to the heirship of the property. However, as they were about giving up the search, Sir George noticed an old trunk lying in a corner, which, his companion told him, had lain there for many a year as lumber, and con-

tained nothing. The Leith Walk gentleman's information
recurring to Sir George, he gave the old moth-eaten chest a
good hearty kick, such as he could wish to have been
received by his " learned friend " the barrister, who spoke
so disrespectfully of his country. The bottom flew out of
the trunk, with a quantity of chaff, among which the original
titles to the property were discovered. Next morning, Sir
George entered the court just as the case was about to be
called and addressed the pretended claimant's counsel—
" Well, sir, what shall I offer you to abandon this action ? "
" No sum, or any consideration whatever, would induce me
to give it up," answered his learned opponent. "Well, sir,"
said Sir George, at the same time pulling out his snuff-horn
and taking a pinch, " I will not even hazard a pinch on it."
The case was called. Sir George, in reply to the claimant's
counsel, in an eloquent speech, addressed the bench ; ex-
posed most effectually the means which had been adopted
to deprive his client of his birthright ; concluded by producing the titles found in the old chest ; and the case was at
once decided in favour of his client. The decision being
announced, Sir George took the young heir's arm, and
bowing to his learned friend the barrister, remarked, " You
see now what a Scotsman has done, and let me tell you that
I wish a countryman of mine anything but a London
barrister." Sir George immediately returned to Edinburgh, well paid for his trouble ; but he never again, in
his favourite walk, encountered the old grey-headed gentleman.

The following two stanzas refer to the Mackenzies of
Kilcoy and their property :—

Nuair a ghlaodhas paisdean tigh Chulchallaidh,
' Tha slige ar mortairean dol thairis ! '
Thig bho Chròidh madadh ruadh
Bhi's 'measg an t-sluaigh mar mhadadh-alluidh,
Rè da-fhichead bliadhna a's corr,
'S gum bi na chòta iomadh mallachd ;
'N sin tilgear e gu falamh brònach
Mar shean sguab air cùl an doruis ;
A's bithidh an tuath mhor mar eunlaith sporsail,
'S an tighearnan cho bochd ris na sporais—
Tha beannachd 'san onair bhoidhich,
A's mallachd an dortadh na fola.

Nuair bhitheas caisteal ciar Chulchallaidh
Na sheasaidh fuar, agus falamh,
'S na cathagan 's na rocuis
Gu seolta sgiathail thairis,
Gabhaidh duine graineal comhnuidh,
Ri thaobh, mi-bheusal a's salach,
Nach gleidh guidhe stal-phosaidh,
'S nach eisd ri cleireach no caraid,
Ach bho Chreag-a-chodh gu Sgire na Toiseachd
Gum bi muisean air toir gach caileag—
A's ochan ! ochan ! s' ma leon,
Sluigidh am balgaire suas moran talamh !

Literally translated :—

When the girls of Kilcoy house cry out,
' The shell (cup) of our murderers is flowing over.'
A fox from Croy will come
Who shall be like a wolf among the people
During forty years and more,
And in his coat shall be many curses ;
He shall then be thrown empty and sorrowful,
Like an old besom behind the door ;

The large farmers will be like sportful birds,
And the lairds as poor as the sparrows—
There's a blessing in handsome honesty
And curses in the shedding of blood.

When the stern Castle of Kilcoy
Shall stand cold and empty,
And the jackdaws and the rooks
Are artfully flying past it,
A loathsome man shall then dwell
Beside it, indecent and filthy,
Who will not keep the vow of the marriage coif,
Listen neither to cleric nor friend ;
But from Creag-a-Chow to Ferrintosh
The dirty fellow will be after every girl—
Ochan ! Ochan ! ! woe's me,
The cunning dog will swallow up much land.

The history of the Kilcoy family has been an unfortunate one in late years, and the second and last lines of the first stanza clearly refer to a well-known tragic incident in the recent history of this once highly-favoured and popular Highland family.

Mr. Maclennan applies them to an earlier event, and says :—" The second and last line of the first stanza refer to the following story—Towards the latter end of the seventeenth century a large number of cattle, in the Black Isle, were attacked with a strange malady, which invariably ended in madness and in death.   The disease was particularly destructive on the Kilcoy and Redcastle estates, and the proprietors offered a large sum of money as a reward to any who should find a remedy.   An old warlock belonging to the parish agreed to protect the cattle from the ravages of this unknown disease, for the sum offered, if they provided him with a human sacrifice.   To this ghastly proposal the lairds agreed.   A large barn at Parkton was, from its secluded position, selected as a suitable place for the horrid crime, where a poor friendless man, who lived at Linwood, close to the site of the present Free Church manse, was requested, under some pretence, to appear on a certain day.   The unsuspecting creature obeyed the summons of his superiors ; he was instantly bound and disem-

E

bowelled alive by the horrid wizard, who dried the heart, liver, kidneys, pancreas, and reduced them to powder, of which he ordered a little to be given to the diseased animals in water. Before the unfortunate victim breathed his last, he ejaculated the following imprecation :—' Gum b' ann nach tig an latha 'bhitheas teaghlach a Chaisteil Ruaidh gun oinseach, na teaghlach Chulchallaidh gun amadan. (Let the day never come when the family of Redcastle shall be without a female idiot, or the family of Kilcoy without a fool.) It appears, not only that this wild imprecation was to some extent realised, but also that the Brahan Seer, years before, knew and predicted that it would be made, and that its prayer would be ultimately granted."

Who the " fox from Croy " is, we are at present unable to suggest; but taking the two stanzas as they stand, it would be difficult to describe the position of the family and the state of the castle, with our present knowledge of their history, and in their present position, more faithfully than Coinneach Odhar has done more than two centuries ago. What a faithful picture of the respective positions of the great farmers and the lairds of the present day ! And what a contrast between their relative positions now and at the time when the Seer predicted the change !

In the appendix to the Life of the late Dr. Norman Macleod, by his brother, the Rev. Donald Macleod, D.D., a series of autobiographical reminiscences are given, which the famous Rev. Norman, the Doctor's father, dictated in his old age to one of his daughters. In the summer of 1799 he visited Dunvegan Castle, the stronghold of the Macleods, in the Isle of Skye. Those of the prophecies already given in verse are, undoubtedly, fragments of the long rhythmical productions of Coinneach Odhar Fiosaiche's prophecies regarding most of our Highland families, to which the Rev. Norman refers, and of which the prophecy given in his reminiscences is as follows :—

" One circumstance took place at the Castle (Dunvegan) on this occasion which I think worth recording, especially as I am the only person now living who can attest the truth of it.   There had been a traditionary prophecy, couched in Gaelic verse, regarding the family of Macleod, which on this occasion, received a most extraordinary fulfilment.   This prophecy I have heard repeated by several persons, and most deeply do I regret that I did not take a copy of it when I could have got it.   The worthy Mr. Campbell of Knock, in Mull, had a very beautiful version of it, as also had my father, and so, I think, had likewise Dr. Campbell of Killinver.   Such prophecies were current regarding almost all old families in the Highlands ; the Argyll family were of the number ; and there is a prophecy regarding the Breadalbane family as yet unfulfilled which I hope may remain so.   The present Marquis of Breadalbane is fully aware of it, as are many of the connections of the family. Of the Macleod family, it was prophesied at least a hundred years prior to the circumstance which I am about to relate.

" In the prophecy to which I am about to allude, it was foretold that when Norman, the Third Norman (' Tormad nan 'tri Tormaid '), the son of the hard-boned English lady (' Mac na mnatha caoile cruaidhe Shassunaich ') would perish by an accidental death ; that when the ' Maidens ' of Macleod (certain well-known rocks on the coast of Macleod's country) became the property of a Campbell ; when a fox had young ones in one of the turrets of the Castle, and particularly when the Fairy enchanted banner should be for the last time exhibited, then the glory of the Macleod family should depart ; a great part of the estate should be sold to others ; so that a small ' curragh,' a boat, would carry all gentlemen of the name of Macleod across Loch Dunvegan; but that in times far distant another John Breac should arise, who should redeem those estates, and raise the power and honours of the house to a higher pitch than ever. Such in general terms was the prophecy. And now as to the curious coincidence of its fulfilment.

"There was, at that time, at Dunvegan, an English smith, with whom I became a favourite, and who told me, in solemn secrecy, that the iron chest which contained the ' fairy flag ' was to be forced open next morning; that he had arranged with Mr. Hector Macdonald Buchanan to be there with his tools for that purpose.

"I was most anxious to be present, and I asked permission to that effect of Mr. Buchanan (Macleod's man of business), who granted me leave on condition that I should not inform anyone of the name of Macleod that such was intended, and should keep it a profound secret from the chief. This I promised and most faithfully acted on. Next morning we proceeded to the chamber in the East Turret, where was the iron chest that contained the famous flag, about which there is an interesting tradition.

"With great violence the smith tore open the lid of this iron chest; but, in doing so, a key was found under part of the covering, which would have opened the chest, had it been found in time. There was an inner case, in which was found the flag, enclosed in a wooden box of strongly-scented wood. The flag consisted of a square piece of very rich silk, with crosses wrought with gold thread, and several elf-spots stitched with great care on different parts of it.

"On this occasion, the melancholy news of the death of the young and promising heir of Macleod reached the Castle. ' Norman, the third Norman, was a lieutenant of H.M.S., the ' Queen Charlotte,' which was blown up at sea, and he and the rest perished. At the same time, the rocks called ' Macleod's Maidens ' were sold, in the course of that very week, to Angus Campbell of Ensay, and they are still in possession of his grandson. A fox in possession of a Lieutenant Maclean, residing in the West Turret of the Castle, had young ones, which I handled, and thus all that was said in the prophecy alluded to was so far fulfilled, although I am glad the family of my chief still enjoy their ancestral possessions, and the worst part of the prophecy accordingly remains unverified. I merely state the facts of the case as they occurred, without expressing any opinion whatever as to the nature of these traditionary legends with which they were connected."

The estates are still, we are glad to say, in possession of the ancient family of Macleod, and the present chief is rapidly improving the prospects of his house. The probabilities are therefore at present against our prophet. The hold of the Macleods on their estates is getting stronger instead of weaker, and the John Breac who is to be the future deliverer has not only not yet appeared, but the undesirable position of affairs requiring his services is yet, we hope, in the distant future.

The Seer predicted that " when the big-thumbed Sheriff-Officer and the blind [man] of the twenty-four fingers shall be together in Barra, Macneil of Barra may be making ready for the flitting " (Nuair a bhitheas maor nan ordagan mora agus dall nan ceithir-meoraibh-fichead comhla ann am Barraidh, faodaidh MacNeill Bharraidh 'bhi deanamh deiseil na h-imirich.) This prediction, which was known in Barra for generations, has been most literally fulfilled. On a certain occasion, " the blind of the twenty-four fingers," so called from having six fingers on each hand, and six toes on each foot, left Benbecula on a tour, to collect alms in South Uist. Being successful there, he decided upon visiting Barra before returning home. Arriving at the Ferry—the isthmus which separates South Uist from Barra—he met " Maor nan Ordagan mora," and they crossed the kyle in the same boat. It was afterwards found that the officer was actually on his way to serve a summons of ejectment on the laird of Barra ; and poor Macneil not only had to make ready for, but had indeed to make the flitting. The man who had acted as guide to the blind on the occasion is, we are informed, still living and in excellent health, though considerably over eighty years of age.

The following is said to have been fulfilled by the conduct of the Duke of Cumberland at and after the battle of Culloden. The Seer was, on one occasion, passing Millburn, on his way from Inverness to Petty, and noticing the old mill, which was a very primitive building, thatched with divots, he said :—" The day will come when thy wheel shall be turned for three successive days by water red with human blood ; for on the banks of thy lade a fierce battle shall be fought, at which much blood shall be spilt." Some say that this is as yet unfulfilled ; and it has been suggested that the battle may yet be fought in connection with the new Barracks now building at the Hut of Health.

Coinneach also prophesied remarkable things regarding the Mackenzies of Fairburn and Fairburn Tower. " The day will come when the Mackenzies of Fairburn shall lose their entire possessions, and that branch of the clan shall disappear almost to a man from the face of the earth. Their Castle shall become uninhabited, desolate, and forsaken, and a cow shall give birth to a calf in the uppermost chamber in Fairburn Tower." The first part of this prophecy has only too literally come to pass ; and within the memory of hundreds now living, and who knew Coinneach's prophecy years before it was fulfilled, the latter part—that referring to the cow calving in the uppermost chamber—has also been undoubtedly realised. We are personally acquainted with people whose veracity is beyond question, who knew the prophecy, and who actually took the trouble at the time to go all the way from Inverness to see the cow-mother and her offspring in the Tower, before they were taken down. Mr. Maclennan supplies the following version —Coinneach said, addressing a large concourse of people—" Strange as it may appear to all those who may hear me this day, yet what I am about to tell you is true and will come to pass at the appointed time. The day will come when a cow shall give birth to a calf in the uppermost chamber (seomar uachdarach) of Fairburn Castle. The child now unborn will see it."

When the Seer uttered this prediction, the Castle of Fairburn was in the possession of, and occupied by, a very rich and powerful chieftain, to whom homage was paid by many of the neighbouring lairds. Its hall rang loud with sounds of music and of mirth, and happiness reigned within its portals. On its winding stone stairs trod and passed carelessly to and fro pages and liveried servants in their wigs and golden trimmings. Nothing in the world was more unlikely to happen, to all appearance, than what the Seer predicted, and Coinneach was universally ridiculed for having given utterance to what was apparently so nonsensical ; but this abuse and ridicule the Seer bore with the patient self-satisfied air of one who was fully convinced of the truth of what he uttered. Years passed by, but no sign of the fulfilment of the prophecy. The Seer, the Laird of Fairburn, and the whole of that generation were gathered to their fathers, and still no signs of the curious prediction

being realised.   The Laird of Fairburn's immediate
successors also followed their predecessors, and the Seer, to
all appearance, was fast losing his reputation as a prophet.
The tower was latterly left uninhabited, and it soon fell into
a dilapidated state of repair—its doors decayed and fell
away from their hinges, one by one, until at last there was
no door on the main stair from the floor to the roof.   Some
years after, and not long ago, the Fairburn tenant-farmer
stored away some straw in the uppermost chamber of the
tower ; in the process, some of the straw dropped, and was
left strewn on the staircase.   One of his cows on a certain
day chanced to find her way to the main door of the tower,
and finding it open, began to pick up the straw scattered
along the stair.   The animal proceeded thus, till she had
actually arrived at the uppermost chamber, whence, being
heavy in calf, she was unable to descend.   She was conse-
quently left in the tower until she gave birth to a fine healthy
calf.   They were allowed to remain there for several days,
where many went to see them, after which the cow and her
progeny were brought down ; and Coinneach Odhar's
prophecy was thus fulfilled to the letter.

" The day will come when the Lewsmen shall go forth
with their hosts to battle, but they will be turned back by
the jaw-bone of an animal smaller than an ass," was a prediction accounted ridiculous and quite incomprehensible
until it was fulfilled in a remarkable but very simple manner.
Seaforth and the leading men of the Clan, as is well known,
were " out in the '15 and '19," and had their estates forfeited ; and it was only a few years before the '45 that their
lands were again restored to Seaforth, and to Mackenzie,
11th Baron of Hilton. The Rev. Colin Mackenzie, a
brother of Hilton, minister of Fodderty and Laird of Glack,
in Aberdeenshire, was the first in the neighbourhood of

Brahan who received information of Prince Charlie's landing in 1745. Seaforth had still a warm feeling for the Prince. His reverend friend, though a thorough Jacobite himself, was an intimate friend of Lord President Forbes, with whom he kept up a regular correspondence. He decided, no doubt mainly through his influence, to remain neutral himself, and fearing that his friend of Brahan might be led to join the Prince, he instantly, on receipt of the news, started for Brahan Castle. Although it was very late at night when he received the information, he crossed Knockfarrel, entered Seaforth's bedroom by the window—for he had already gone to rest for the night—and without awakening his lady, informed him of the landing of Charles. They decided upon getting out of the way, and both immediately disappeared. Seaforth was well known to have had previous correspondence with the Prince, and to have sent private orders to the Lews to have his men there in readiness ; and Fodderty impressed upon him the prudence of getting out of sight altogether in the meantime. They started through the mountains in the direction of Poolewe, and some time afterwards, when there together in concealment near the shore, they saw two ships entering the bay, having on board a large number of armed men, whom they at once recognised as Seaforth's followers from the Lews, raised and commanded by Captain Colin Mackenzie, the great-grandfather of Major Thomas Mackenzie of the 78th Highlanders. Lord Seaforth had just been making a repast of a sheep's head, when he espied his retainers, and approaching the ships with the sheep's jaw-bone in his hand, he waved it towards them, and ordered them to return to their homes at once, which command they obeyed by making at once for Stornoway ; and thus was fulfilled Coinneach Odhar's apparently ludicrous prediction, that the brave Lewsmen would be turned back from battle with the jaw-bone of an animal smaller than an ass.

Mr. Maclennan supplies us also with the following :—"In the parish of Avoch is a well of beautiful clear water, out of which the Brahan Seer, upon one occasion, took a refreshing draught. So pleased was he with the water, that he looked at his Blue Stone, and said—' Whoever he be that drinketh of thy water henceforth, if suffering from any disease, shall, by placing two pieces of straw or wood on thy surface, ascertain whether he will recover or not. If he is to recover, the straw will whirl round in opposite directions; if he is to die soon, they will remain stationary.' The writer (continues Mr. Maclennan) knew people who went to the well and made the experiment. He was himself once unwell, and supposed to be at the point of death; he got of the water of the well, and he still lives. Whether it did him good or not, it is impossible to say, but this he does know, that the water pleased him uncommonly well."

With reference to Lady Hill, in the same parish, the Seer said—" Thy name has gone far and wide; but though thy owners were brave on the field of battle, they never decked thy brow. The day will come, however, when a white collar shall be put upon thee. The child that is unborn shall see it, but I shall not." This prediction has been fulfilled a few years ago, by the construction of a fine drive right round the hill.

The Seer said, speaking of Beauly—" The day will come, however distant, when ' Cnoc na Rath ' will be in the centre of the village." It certainly would appear incredible, and even absurd, to suggest such a thing in Coinneach's day, for the " village " then stood at a place south of the present railway station, called, in Gaelic, " Bealaidh-Achadh," or the Broom field, quite a mile from Cnoc na Rath. The

prophecy has to some extent been fulfilled, for the last
erection at Beauly—the new public school—is within a few
yards of the Cnoc ; and the increasing enterprise of the
inhabitants is rapidly aiding, and, indeed, will soon secure,
the absolute realisation of the Seer's prediction.   In connection with this prophecy we think that we have discovered
a Celtic origin for the term Beauly.   It is generally supposed
to have been derived from the French word " Beaulieu."
The village being originally at Bealaidh-Achadh," and so
called when the present Beauly was nowhere, what can be
more natural than the supposition that the inhabitants
carried the original name of their original village along with
them, and now present us with the Gaelic " Bealaidh,"
anglified into Beauly.   This is not such a fine theory as
the French one, but it is more likely to be the true one, and
is more satisfactory to the student of Gaelic topography.

We have several versions of the prophecy regarding the
carrying away of the Stone Bridge across the River Ness,
which stood near the place where the present Suspension
Bridge stands.   Mr. Macintyre supplies the following, and
Mr. Maclennan's version is very much the same :—" He
foretold that the Ness Bridge would be swept away by a
great flood, while crowded with people, and while a man
riding a white horse and a woman ' enciente ' were crossing
it.   Either the prophet's second-sight failed him on the
occasion, or tradition has not preserved the correct version
of the prediction, for it is well known that no human being
was carried away by the bridge when it was swept away by
the extraordinary flood of 1849."

As a matter of fact, there was no man riding a white
horse on the bridge at the time, but a man—Matthew
Campbell—and a woman were crossing it, the arches tumbl-
ing one by one at their heels as they flew across ; but they

managed to reach the western shore in safety, just as the
last arch was crumbling under their feet.   Campbell, who
was behind, coming up to the woman, caught her in his
arms, and with a desperate bound cleared the crumbling
structure.

The Seer also foretold that before the latter prediction
was fulfilled " people shall pick gooseberries from a bush
growing on the stone ledge of one of the arches."   There
are many now living who remember this gooseberry bush,
and who have seen it in bloom and blossom, and with fruit
upon it.   It grew on the south side of the bridge, on the
third or fourth pier, and near the iron grating which supplied
a dismal light to the dungeon which in those days was the
Inverness prison.   Maclean, " A Nonagenarian," writing
forty years ago, says nothing of the bush, but, while writing
of the predicted fall of the bridge, states with regard to it.
that " an old tradition or prophecy is, that many lives will
be lost at its fall, and that this shall take place when there
are seven females on the bridge, in a state poetically described as that ' in which ladies wish to be who love their
lords.' "   This was written, as will be seen by comparing
dates, several years before the bridge was carried away in
1849, showing unmistakably that the prophecy was not
concocted after the event.

" The natural arch, or ' Clach tholl,' near Storehead in
Assynt, will fall with a crash so loud as to cause the laird
of Leadmore's cattle, twenty miles away, to break their
tethers."   This was fulfilled in 1841, Leadmore's cattle
having one day strayed from home to within a few hundred
yards of the arch, when it fell with such a crash as to send
them home in a frantic fright, tearing everything before
them.   Hugh Miller refers to this prediction, as also to
several others, in the work already alluded to—" Scenes

and Legends of the North of Scotland," pp. 161, 162, 163.

About sixteen years ago, there lived in the village of " Baile Mhuilinn," in the West of Sutherlandshire, an old woman of about ninety-five years of age, known as Baraball n'ic Coinnich (Annabella Mackenzie). From her position, history, and various personal peculiarities, it was universally believed in the district that she was no other than the Baraball n'ic Coinnich of whom the Brahan Seer predicted that she would die of the measles. She had, however, arrived at such an advanced age, without any appearance or likelihood of her ever having that disease, that the prophet was rapidly losing credit in the district. About this time the measles had just gone the round of the place, and had made considerable havoc among old and young ; but when the district was, so to speak, convalescent, the measles paid Baraball a visit, and actually carried her away, when within a few years of five score, leaving no doubt whatever in the minds of the people that she had died as foretold centuries before by the famous Coinneach Odhar.

The Seer, one day, pointing to the now celebrated Strath-peffer mineral wells, said :—" Uninviting and disagreeable as it now is, with its thick crusted surface and unpleasant smell, the day will come when it shall be under lock and key, and crowds of pleasure and health seekers shall be seen thronging its portals, in their eagerness to get a draught of its waters."

Regarding the " land-grasping " Urquharts of Cromarty he predicted " that, extensive though their possessions in the Black Isle now are, the day will come—and it is close at hand—when they will not own twenty acres in the district." This, like many of his other predictions, literally came to pass, although nothing could then have been more unlikely; for, at the time, the Urquharts possessed the estates of Kinbeachie, Braelangwell, Newhall, and Monteagle, but at this moment their only possession in the Black Isle is a small piece of Braelangwell.

That " the day will come when fire and water shall run in streams through all the streets and lanes of Inverness," was a prediction, the fulfilment of which was quite incomprehensible, until the introduction of gas and water through pipes into every corner of the town.

" The day will come when long strings of carriages without horses shall run between Dingwall and Inverness, and more wonderful still, between Dingwall and the Isle of Skye." It is hardly necessary to point out that this refers to the railway carriages now running in those districts.

That " a bald black girl will be born at the back of the Church of Gairloch " (Beirear nighean mhaol dubh air cùl Eaglais Ghearrloch), has been fulfilled. During one of the usual large gatherings at the Sacramental Communion a well-known young woman was taken in labour, and before she could be removed she gave birth to the " nighean mhaol dubh," whose descendants are well known and pointed out in the district to this day as the fulfilment of Coinneach's prophecy.

That " a white cow will give birth to a calf in the garden behind Gairloch House," has taken place within the memory of people still living ; that, in Fowerdale, " a black hornless cow (Bo mhaol dubh) will give birth to a calf with two heads," happened within our own recollection. These predictions were well known to people before they came to pass.

The following are evidently fragments regarding the Lovat Estates. He said :—

Thig fear tagair bho dheas,
Mar eun bho phreas.
Fasaidh e mar luibh,
'S sgaoilidh e mar shiol,
'S cuiridh e teine ri Ardrois.

(A Claimant will come from the South
Like a bird from a bush ;
He will grow like an herb ;
He will spread like seed,
And set fire to Ardross.)*

" Mhac Shimidh ball-dubh, a dh'fhagus an oighreachd gun an t-oighre dligheach." (Mac Shimidh (Lovat), the black-spotted, who will leave the Estate without the rightful heir.) " An Sisealach claon ruadh, a dh'fhagus an oighreachd gun an t-oighre dligheach." (Chisholm, the squint-eyed, who will leave the estate without the rightful heir.) " An tighearna stòrach a dh'fhagus oighreachd Ghearrloch gun an t-oighre dligheach." (The buck-toothed laird who will leave the estate of Gairloch without the rightful heir), are also fragments.

We do not know whether there has been any Lovat or Chisholm with the peculiar personal characteristics mentioned by the Seer, †and shall be glad to receive information on the point, as well as a fuller and more particular version of the prophecy. We are aware, however, that Sir Hector Mackenzie of Gairloch was buck-toothed, and that he was always known among his tenants in the west, as " An

---

*A place of that name near Beauly.

†Since the above was in type, we came across the following in Anderson's History of the Family of Fraser, p. 114 :—" Hugh, son of the 10th Lord Lovat, was born on the 28th September, 1666. From a large black spot on his upper lip he was familiarly called, Mac Shimidh Ball-dubh, i.e., black-spotted Simpson or Lovat. Three chieftains were distinguished at this time by similar deformities—(1) MacCoinnich Glùn-dubh, i.e., black-kneed Mackenzie ; (2) Macintoshich Claon, i.e., squint-eyed MacKintosh; Sisealach Càm, crooked or one-eyed Chisholm."

tighearna stòrach." We heard old people maintaining that Coinneach was correct even in this instance, and that his prediction has been actually fulfilled ; but, at present, we abstain from going into that part of this family history which would throw light on the subject. A gentleman is trying to assert rights to the Lovat estates at the present moment.

Before proceeding to give such of the prophecies regarding the family of Seaforth as have been so literally fulfilled in the later annals of that once great and powerful house—the history of the family being so intimately interwoven with, and being itself really the fulfilment of the Seer's predictions—it may interest the reader to have a cursory glance at it from the earliest period in which the family appears in history.

SKETCH OF THE FAMILY OF SEAFORTH.

THE most popularly-received theory regarding the Mackenzies is that they are descended from an Irishman of the name of Colinas Fitzgerald, son of the Earl of Kildare or Desmond, who distinguished himself by his bravery at the battle of Largs in 1263. It is said that his courage and valour were so singularly distinguished that King Alexander the Third took him under his special protection, and granted him a charter of the lands of Kintail, in Wester Ross, bearing date from Kincardine, January the 9th, 1263.

According to the fragmentary " Record of Icolmkill," upon which the claim of the Irish origin of the clan is founded, a personage, described as " Peregrinus et Hibernus nobilis ex familia Geraldinorum "—that is " a noble stranger and Hibernian, of the family of the Geraldines "—being driven from Ireland with a considerable number of his followers was, about 1261, very graciously received by the King, and afterwards remained at his court. Having given powerful aid to the Scots at the Battle of Largs, two years afterwards he was rewarded by a grant of the lands of Kintail, which were erected into a free barony by royal charter, dated as above mentioned. Mr. Skene, however, says that no such document as this Icolmkill Fragment was ever known to exist, as nobody has ever seen it ; and as for Alexander's charter, he declares (Highlanders, vol. ii., p. 235) that it " bears the most palpable marks of having been a forgery of a later date, and one by no means happy in the execution." Besides, the words " Colino Hiberno " contained in it do not prove this Colin to have been an Irishman, as Hiberni was at that period a common appellation for the Gael of Scotland. Burke, in the " Peerage " has adopted the Irish origin of the clan, and the chiefs themselves seem to have adopted this theory, without having made any particular inquiry as to whether it was well founded or not. The Mackenzie chiefs were thus not exempt from the almost universal, but most unpatriotic, fondness exhibited by many other Highland chiefs for a foreign origin. In examining the traditions of our country, we are forcibly struck with this peculiarity of taste. Highlanders despising a Caledonian source trace their ancestors from Ireland, Norway, Sweden, or Normandy. The progenitors of the Mackenzies can be traced with greater certainty, and with no less claim to antiquity, from a native ancestor, Gillean (Cailean) Og, or Colin the Younger, a son of Cailean na h'Airde, ancestor of the Earls of Ross ; and, from the MS. of 1450, their Gaelic descent may now be considered beyond dispute.*

Until the forfeiture of the Lords of the Isles, the Mackenzies always held their lands from the Earls of Ross, and followed their banner in the field, but after the forfeiture of the great and powerful earldom, the Mackenzies rapidly rose on the ruins of the Macdonalds to the great power, extent of territorial possession, and almost regal magnificence for which they were afterwards distinguished among the other great clans of the north. They, in the reign of James the First, acquired a very powerful influence in the

*See Nos. XXVI. and XXVII. of the *Celtic Magazine*, Vol. III., in which this question is discussed at length.

Highlands, and became independent of any superior but the Crown. Mackenzie and his followers were, in fact, about the most potent chief and clan in the whole Highlands.

Kenneth, son of Angus, is supposed to have commenced his rule in Kintail about 1278, and was succeeded by his son, John, in 1304, who was in his turn succeeded by his son, Kenneth. John, Kenneth's son, was called Iain Mac-Choinnich, John MacKenneth, or John son of Kenneth, hence the family name Mackenny or Mackenzie. The name Kenneth in course of time became softened down to Kenny or Kenzie. It is well known that, not so very long ago, *z* in this and all other names continued to be of the same value as the letter *y*, just as we still find it in Menzies, MacFadzean, and many others. There seems to be no doubt whatever that this is the real origin of the Mackenzies, and of their name.

Murchadh, or Murdo, son of Kenneth, it is said, received a charter of the lands of Kintail from David II.

In 1463, Alexander Mackenzie of Kintail obtained the lands of Strathgarve, and other possessions, from John, Earl of Ross. They afterwards strenuously and successfully opposed every attempt made by the Macdonalds to obtain possession of the forfeited earldom. Alexander was succeeded by his son, Kenneth, who married Lady Margaret Macdonald, daughter of the forfeited Earl John, Lord of the Isles ; but through some cause,* Mackenzie divorced the lady, and sent her home in a most ignominious and degrading manner. She had only one eye, and Kintail sent her home riding a one-eyed steed, accompanied by a

---

*For full details of this act, which afterwards proved the cause of such strife and bloodshed, see Mackenzie's " History of the Clan Mackenzie."

one-eyed servant, followed by a one-eyed dog. All these circumstances exasperated the lady's family to such an extent as to make them ever after the mortal and sworn enemies of the Mackenzies.

Kenneth Og, his son by the divorced wife, became chief in 1493. Two years afterwards, he and Farquhar Mackintosh were imprisoned by James V. in Edinburgh Castle. In 1497, however, they both made their escape, but were, on their way to the Highlands, seized in a most treacherous manner, at Torwood, by the laird of Buchanan. Kenneth Og made a stout resistance, but he was ultimately slain, and Buchanan sent his head as a present to the King.

Leaving no issue, Kenneth was succeeded by his brother John, whose mother, Agnes Fraser, his father's second wife, was a daughter of Lovat. He had several other sons, from whom have sprung other branches of the Mackenzies. As John was very young, his uncle, Hector Roy (Eachainn Ruadh) Mackenzie, progenitor of the house of Gairloch, assumed command of the clan and the guardianship of the young chief. Gregory informs us, that " under his rule the Clan Kenzie became involved in feuds with the Munroes and other clans ; and Hector Roy himself became obnoxious to the Government as a disturber of the public peace. His intentions towards the young chief of Kintail were considered very dubious, and the apprehensions of the latter and his friends having been roused, Hector was compelled by law to yield up the estate and the command of the tribe to the proper heir."* John, the lawful heir, on obtaining possession, at the call of James IV., marched at the head of his clan to the fatal field of Flodden, where he was made prisoner by the English, but afterwards escaped.

*Highlands and Isles of Scotland, p. 111.

On King James the Fifth's expedition to the Western Isles in 1540, John joined him at Kintail, and accompanied him throughout his whole journey.   He fought with his clan at the battle of Pinkie in 1547, and died in 1561, when he was succeeded by his son, Kenneth, who had two sons by a daughter of the Earl of Athole—Colin and Roderick—the latter becoming ancestor of the Mackenzies of Redcastle, Kincraig, Rosend, and several other branches.   This Colin, who was the eleventh chief, fought for Queen Mary at the battle of Langside.   He was twice married.   By his first wife, Barbara Grant of Grant—whose elopement with him will be found described in a poem in the *Highland Ceilidh*, Vol I., pp. 215-220, of the *Celtic Magazine*—he had four sons and three daughters, namely—Kenneth, who became his successor ; Sir Roderick Mackenzie of Tarbat, ancestor of the Earls of Cromartie ; Colin, ancestor of the Mackenzies of Kennock and Pitlundie ; and Alexander, ancestor of the Mackenzies of Kilcoy, and other families of the name. By Mary, eldest daughter of Roderick Mackenzie of Davochmaluag, he had a natural son, Alexander, from whom descended the Mackenzies of Applecross, Coul, Delvin, Assynt, and others of note in history.

Kenneth, the eldest son, soon after succeeding his father, was engaged in supporting Torquil Macleod of Lewis, surnamed the " Conanach," the disinherited son of the Macleod of Lewis, and who was closely related to himself. Torquil conveyed the barony of Lewis to the Chief of the Mackenzies by formal deed, the latter causing the usurper to the estate, and his followers, to be beheaded in 1597.   He afterwards, in the following year, joined Macleod of Harris and Macdonald of Sleat, in opposing James the Sixth's project for the colonisation of the Lewis by the well-known adventurers from the " Kingdom of Fife."

In 1602, the old and long-standing feud between the Mackenzies and the Macdonalds of Glengarry, concerning their lands in Wester Ross, was renewed with infuriated violence. Ultimately, after great bloodshed and carnage on both sides, an arrangement was arrived at by which Glengarry renounced for ever, in favour of Mackenzie, the Castle of Strome and all his lands in Lochalsh, Lochcarron, and other places in the vicinity, so long the bone of contention between these powerful and ferocious chieftains. In 1607, a Crown charter for these lands was granted to Kenneth, thus materially adding to his previous possessions, power, and influence. " All the Highlands and Isles, from Ardna-murchan to Strathnaver, were either the Mackenzies' pro-perty or under their vassalage, some few excepted," and all around them were bound to them " by very strict bonds of friendship." In this same year Kenneth received, through some influence at Court, a gift, under the Great Seal, of the Island of Lewis, in virtue of, and thus confirming, the resig-nation of this valuable and extensive property previously made in his favour by Torquil Macleod. A complaint was, however, made to his Majesty by those of the colonists who survived, and Mackenzie was again forced to resign it. By patent, dated the 19th of November, 1609, he was created a peer of the realm, as Lord Mackenzie of Kintail. Soon after, the colonies gave up all hopes of being able to colonize the Lewis, and the remaining adventurers—Sir George Hay and Sir James Spens—were easily prevailed upon to sell their rights to Lord Mackenzie, who at the same time succeeded in securing a grant from the king of that part of the island forfeited by Lord Balmerino, another of the adventurers. He (Lord Mackenzie) now secured a commission of fire and sword against the islanders, soon arrived with a strong force, and speedily reduced them to obedience, with the exception of Neil Macleod and a few of his followers. The struggle between these two continued for a time, but ultimately Mackenzie managed to obtain possession of the whole island, and it remained in the possession of the family until it was sold by the " Last of the Seaforths."

This, the first, Lord Mackenzie of Kintail died in 1611. One of his sons, Simon Mackenzie of Lochslin, by his second wife, Isabella, daughter of Sir Alexander Ogilvie of Powrie, was the father of the celebrated Sir George Mackenzie, already referred to. His eldest son, Colin, who succeeded him as second Lord Mackenzie of Kintail, was created first Earl of Seaforth, by patent dated the 3rd December, 1623, to himself and his heirs male. Kenneth, Colin's grandson, and third Earl of Seaforth, distinguished himself by his loyalty to Charles the Second during the Commonwealth. He supported the cause of the Royalists so long as there was an opportunity of fighting for it in the field, and when forced to submit to the ruling powers, he was committed to prison, where, with much firmness of mind and nobility of soul, he endured a tedious captivity during many years, until he was ultimately released, after the Restoration, by authority of the king. He married a lady descended from a branch of his own family, Isabella Mackenzie, daughter of Sir John Mackenzie of Tarbat, and sister of the first Earl of Cromartie. To her cruel and violent conduct may undoubtedly be traced the remarkable doom which awaited the family of Seaforth, which was predicted in such an extraordinary manner by Coinneach Odhar, fulfilled in its minutest details, and which we are, in the following pages, to place before the reader.

SEAFORTH'S DREAM.

BEFORE proceeding to relate the Seer's remarkable prediction, and the extraordinary minuteness with which it has been fulfilled, we shall give the particulars of a curious dream by Lord Seaforth, which was a peculiar forecast of the loss of his faculties of speech and hearing during the latter part of his eventful life. It has been supplied by a member of the family,* who shows an unmistakable interest in everything calculated to throw light on the " prophecies," and who evidently believes them not to be merely an old wife's tale. We give it *verbatim et literatim :*—" The last Lord Seaforth was born in full possession of all his faculties. When about twelve years of age scarlet fever broke out in the school at which he was boarding. All the boys who were able to be sent away were returned to their homes at once, and some fifteen or twenty boys who had taken the infection were moved into a large room, and there treated. After a week had passed, some boys naturally became worse than others, and some of them were in great danger. One evening, before dark, the attendant nurse, having left the dormitory, for a few minutes, was alarmed by a cry. She instantly returned, and found Lord Seaforth in a state of great excitement. After he became calmer, he told the nurse that he

---

*The late Colonel John Constantine Stanley, son of Lord Stanley of Alderley, who married Susan Mary, eldest daughter of the late Keith William Stewart Mackenzie of Seaforth.

had seen, soon after she had left the room, the door opposite to his bed silently open, and a hideous old woman came in. She had a wallet full of something hanging from her neck in front of her. She paused on entering, then turned to the bed close to the door, and stared steadily at one of the boys lying in it. She then passed to the foot of the next boy's bed, and, after a moment, stealthily moved up to the head, and taking from her wallet a mallet and peg, drove the peg into his forehead. Young Seaforth said he heard the crash of the bones, though the boy never stirred. She then proceeded round the room, looking at some boys longer than at others. When she came to him, his suspense was awful. He felt he could not resist or even cry out, and he never could forget, in years after, that moment's agony, when he saw her hand reaching down for a nail, and feeling his ears. At last, after a look, she slunk off, and slowly completing the circuit of the room, disappeared noiselessly through the same door by which she had entered. Then he felt the spell seemed to be taken off, and uttered the cry which had alarmed the nurse. The latter laughed at the lad's story, and told him to go to sleep. When the doctor came, an hour later, to make his rounds, he observed that the boy was feverish and excited, and asked the nurse afterwards if she knew the cause, whereupon she reported what had occurred. The doctor, struck with the story, returned to the boy's bedside and made him repeat his dream. He took it down in writing at the moment. The following day nothing eventful happened, but, in course of time, some got worse, a few indeed died, others suffered but slightly, while some, though they recovered, bore some evil trace and consequence of the fever for the rest of their lives. The doctor, to his horror, found that those whom Lord Seaforth had described as having

a peg driven into their foreheads, were those who died from
the fever; those whom the old hag passed by recovered,
and were none the worse; whereas those she appeared to
look at intently, or handled, all suffered afterwards. Lord
Seaforth left his bed of sickness almost stone deaf; and, in
later years, grieving over the loss of his four sons, absolutely
and entirely ceased to speak.

We shall now relate the circumstances connected with
the prophecy, and continue an account of the Seaforth's
connection with it to the end of the chapter.

SEAFORTH'S DOOM.

KENNETH, the third Earl, had occasion to visit Paris on some business after the Restoration of King Charles the Second, and after having secured his liberty. He left the Countess at Brahan Castle, unattended by her lord, and, as she thought, forgotten, while he was enjoying the dissipations and amusements of the French capital, which seemed to have many attractions for him, for he prolonged his stay far beyond his original intention. Lady Seaforth had become very uneasy concerning his prolonged absence, more especially as she received no letters from him for several months. Her anxiety became too strong for her power of endurance, and led her to have recourse to the services of the local prophet. She accordingly sent messages to Strathpeffer, summoning Coinneach to her presence, to obtain from him, if possible, some tidings of her absent lord. Coinneach, as we have seen, was already celebrated, far and wide, throughout the whole Highlands, for his great powers of divination, and his relations with the invisible world.

Obeying the orders of Lady Seaforth, Kenneth arrived at the Castle, and presented himself to the Countess, who required him to give her information concerning her absent lord. Coinneach asked where Seaforth was supposed to be, and said, that he thought he would be able to find him if he was still alive. He applied the divination stone to his eye, and laughed loudly, saying to the Countess, " Fear not for your lord, he is safe and sound, well and hearty, merry and happy." Being now satisfied that her husband's life was safe, she wished Kenneth to describe his appearance; to tell her where he was now engaged, and all his surroundings. " Be satisfied," he said, " ask no questions, let it suffice you to know that your lord is well and merry." " But," demanded the lady, " where is he? with whom is he? and is he making any preparations for coming home? " " Your lord," replied the seer, " is in a magnificent room, in very fine company, and far too agreeably employed at present to think of leaving Paris." The Countess, finding that her lord was well and happy, began to fret that she had no share in his happiness and amusements, and to feel even the pangs of jealousy and wounded pride. She thought there was something in the seer's looks and expression which seemed to justify such feelings. He spoke sneeringly and maliciously of her husband's occupations, as much as to say, that he could tell a disagreeable tale if he would. The lady tried entreaties, bribes, and threats to induce Coinneach to give a true account of her husband, as he had seen him, to tell who was with him, and all about him. Kenneth pulled himself together, and proceeded to say—" As you will know that which will make you unhappy, I must tell you the truth. My lord seems to have little thought of you, or of his children, or of his Highland home. I saw him in a gay-gilded room, grandly decked out in velvets, with silks and cloth of gold, and on his knees before a fair lady, his arm round her waist, and her hand pressed to his lips." At this unexpected and painful disclosure, the rage of the lady knew no bounds. It was natural and well merited, but its object was a mistake. All the anger which ought to have been directed against her husband, and which should have been concentrated in her breast, to be poured out upon him after his return, was spent upon poor Coinneach Odhar. She felt the more keenly, that the disclosures of her husband's infidelity had not been made to herself in private, but in the presence of the principal retainers of her house, so that the Earl's moral character was blasted, and her own charms slighted, before the whole clan; and her husband's desertion of her for a French lady was certain to become the public scandal of all the North of Scotland. She formed a sudden resolution with equal presence of mind and cruelty. She determined to discredit the revelations of the seer, and to denounce him as a vile slanderer of her husband's character. She trusted that the signal vengeance she was about to inflict upon him as a liar and defamer would impress the minds, not only of her own clan, but of all the inhabitants of the counties of Ross and Inverness, with a sense of her thorough disbelief in the scandalous story, to which she nevertheless secretly attached full credit. Turning to the seer, she said, " You have spoken evil of dignities, you have vilified the mighty of the land ; you have defamed a mighty chief in the midst of his vassals, you have abused my hospitality and outraged my feelings, you have sullied the good name of my lord in the halls of his ancestors, and you shall suffer the most signal vengeance I can inflict— you shall suffer the death."

Coinneach was filled with astonishment and dismay at this fatal result of his art. He had expected far other rewards from his art of divination. However, he could not at first believe the rage of the Countess to be serious; at all events, he expected that it would soon evaporate, and that, in the course of a few hours, he would be allowed to depart in peace. He even so far understood her feelings that he thought she was making a parade of anger in order to discredit the report of her lord's shame before the clan;

and he expected that when this object was served, he might at length be dismissed without personal injury. But the decision of the Countess was no less violently conceived than it was promptly executed. The doom of Coinneach was sealed. No time was to be allowed for remorseless compunction. No preparation was permitted to the wretched man. No opportunity was given for intercession in his favour. The miserable seer was led out for immediate execution.

Such a stretch of feudal oppression, at a time so little remote as the reign of Charles II., may appear strange. A castle may be pointed out, however, viz., Menzies Castle, much less remote from the seat of authority, and the Courts of Law, than Brahan, where, half a century later, an odious vassal was starved to death by order of the wife of the chief, the sister of the great and patriotic Duke of Argyll!

When Coinneach found that no mercy was to be expected either from the vindictive lady or her subservient vassals, he resigned himself to his fate. He drew forth his white stone, so long the instrument of his supernatural intelligence, and once more applying it to his eye, said—" I see into the far future, and I read the doom of the race of my oppressor. The long-descended line of Seaforth will, ere many generations have passed, end in extinction and in sorrow. I see a chief, the last of his house, both deaf and dumb. He will be the father of four fair sons, all of whom he will follow to the tomb. He will live careworn and die mourning, knowing that the honours of his line are to be extinguished for ever, and that no future chief of the Mackenzies shall bear rule at Brahan or in Kintail. After lamenting over the last and most promising of his sons, he himself shall sink into the grave, and the remnant of his possessions shall be inherited by a white-coifed (or white-hooded) lassie from the

East, and she is to kill her sister. And as a sign by which it may be known that these things are coming to pass, there shall be four great lairds in the days of the last deaf and dumb Seaforth—Gairloch, Chisholm, Grant, and Raasay—of whom one shall be buck-toothed, another hare-lipped, another half-witted, and the fourth a stammerer. Chiefs distinguished by these personal marks shall be the allies and neighbours of the last Seaforth; and when he looks around him and sees them, he may know that his sons are doomed to death, that his broad lands shall pass away to the stranger, and that his race shall come to an end."

When the seer had ended his prediction, he threw his white stone into a small loch, and declared that whoever should find that stone would be similarly gifted. Then, submitting to his fate, he was at once executed, and this wild and fearful doom ended his strange and uncanny life.

Sir Bernard Burke, to whose " Vicissitudes of Families " we are mainly indebted for this part of the Prophecies, says :—With regard to the four Highland lairds, who were to be buck-toothed, hare-lipped, half-witted, and a stammerer—Mackenzie, Baronet of Gairloch; Chisholm of Chisholm; Grant, Baronet of Grant; and Macleod of Raasay—I am uncertain which was which. Suffice it to say, that the four lairds were marked by the above-mentioned distinguishing personal peculiarities, and all four were the contemporaries of the last of the Seaforths.

We believe Sir Hector Mackenzie of Gairloch was the buck-toothed laird (an Tighearna Stòrach); the Chisholm, the hare-lipped; Grant, the half-witted; and Raasay, the stammerer, all of whom were contemporaries of the last Lord Seaforth.

THE SEER'S DEATH.

M R. MACINTYRE supplies the following account of the Seaforth prophecy and the Seer's death, as related at this day, in the Black Isle :—

Coinneach's supernatural power was at length the cause which led to his untimely and cruel death. At a time when there was a convivial gathering in Brahan Castle, a large concourse of local aristocratic guests was present. As the youthful portion were amusing themselves in the beautiful grounds or park surrounding the castle, and displaying their noble forms and features as they thought to full advantage, a party remarked in Coinneach Odhar's hearing, that such a gathering of gentlemen's children could rarely be seen. The seer answered with a sneer, " that he saw more in the company of the children of footmen and grooms than of the children of gentlemen," (Is mo th'ann do chlann ghillean-buird agus do chlann ghillean-stabuil na th'ann do chlann dhaoin' uaisle,) a remark which soon came to the ears of Lady Seaforth and the other ladies present, who were so much offended and provoked at this base insinuation as to the paternity of the Brahan guests, that they determined at once to have condign punishment on the once respected seer. He was forthwith ordered to be seized ; and, after eluding the search of his infuriated pursuers for some time, was at last apprehended. Seeing he had no way of escape, he once more applied the magic stone to his eye, and uttered the well-known prophetic curse [already given] against the Brahan family, and then threw the stone into a cow's footmark, which was full of water, declaring that a child would be born with two navels, or as some say, with four thumbs and six toes, who would in course of time discover it inside a pike, and who then would be gifted with Coinneach's prophetic power. As it was the purpose of his pursuers to obtain possession of this wonderful stone, as well as of the prophet's person, search was eagerly made for it in the muddy waters in the footprint, when, lo ! it was found that more water was copiously oozing from the boggy ground around, and rapidly forming a considerable lake, that effectually concealed the much-coveted stone. The waters steadily increased, and the result, as the story goes, was the formation of Loch Ussie (Oozie). The poor prophet was then taken to Chanonry Point, where the stern arm of ecclesiastical authority, with unrelenting severity, burnt him to death in a tar-barrel for witchcraft.

It is currently reported that a person answering to the foregoing description was actually born in the neighbourhood of Conon, near Loch Ussie, and is still living. Of this I have been credibly informed by a person who saw him several times at the Muir of Ord markets.

We see from the public prints, our correspondent humorously continues, that the Magistrates and Police Commissioners of Dingwall contemplate to bring a supply of water for " Baile-'Chail " from Loch Ussie. Might we humbly suggest with such a view in prospect, as some comfort to the burdened ratepayers, that there may be, to say the least, a probability in the course of such an undertaking of recovering the mystic stone, so long compelled to hide its prophetic light in the depths of Loch Ussie, and so present

G

the world with the novel sight of having not only an indivi-
dual gifted with second-sight, but also a Corporation ; and,
further, what would be a greater terror to evil-doers, a
magistracy capable, in the widest sense of the word, of dis-
cerning between right and wrong, good and evil, and thus
compelling the lieges in the surrounding towns and villages
to exclaim involuntarily—*O si sic omnes !* They might go
the length even of lending it out, and giving you the use
of it occasionally in Inverness.

When Coinneach Odhar was being led to the stake, fast
bound with cords, Lady Seaforth exultingly declared that,
having had so much unhallowed intercourse with the unseen
world, he would never go to Heaven.   But the seer, looking
round upon her with an eye from which his impending fate
had not banished the ray of a joyful hope of rest in a future
state, gravely answered—" *I* will go to Heaven, but *you*
never shall ; and this will be a sign whereby you can
determine whether my condition after death is one of ever-
lasting happiness or of eternal misery ; a raven and a dove,
swiftly flying in opposite directions will meet, and for a
second hover over my ashes, on which they will instantly
alight.   If the raven be foremost, you have spoken truly ;
but if the dove, then my hope is well-founded."   And,
accordingly, tradition relates, that after the cruel sentence of
his hard-hearted enemies had been executed upon the
Brahan Seer, and his ashes lay scattered among the
smouldering embers of the fagot, his last prophecy was most
literally fulfilled ; for those messengers, emblematically
denoting—the one sorrow, the other joy—came speeding to
the fatal spot, when the dove, with characteristic flight,
closely followed by the raven, darted downwards and was
first to alight on the dust of the departed Coinneach Odhar ;
thus completely disproving the positive and uncharitable

assertion of the proud and vindictive Lady of Brahan, to the wonder and consternation of all the beholders.

Mr. Maclennan describes the cause of Coinneach's doom in almost identical terms ; the only difference being, that while the former has the young ladies amusing themselves on the green outside, the latter describes them having a grand dance in the great hall of the Castle. The following is his account of the prophet's end :—

In terms of her expressed resolution, Lady Seaforth, some days after this magnificent entertainment, caused the seer to be seized, bound hand and foot, and carried forthwith to the Ness of Chanonry, where, despite his pitiful looks and lamentable cries, he was inhumanly thrown, head foremost, into a barrel of burning tar, the inside of which was thickly studded with sharp and long spikes driven in from the outside. On the very day upon which Coinneach was sent away from the castle to meet his cruel fate, Lord Seaforth arrived, and was immediately informed of his lady's resolution, and that Coinneach was already well on his way to the Chanonry, where he was to be burned that very day, under the vindictive and cruel nature of his Countess, believed the story to be only too true. He waited neither for food nor refreshment ; called neither for groom nor for servant, but hastened immediately to the stable, saddled his favourite steed with his own hands, for lairds were not so proud in those days, and set off at full speed, hoping to reach Chanonry Point before the diabolical intention of her ladyship and her religious (!) advisers should be carried into effect. Never before nor since did Seaforth ride so furiously as he did on that day. He was soon at Fortrose, when he observed a dense smoke rising higher and higher from the promontory below. He felt his whole frame giving way, and a cold sweat came over his body, for he felt that the foul deed was, or was about to be, perpetrated.   He pulled himself together, however, and with fresh energy and redoubled vigour, spurred his steed, which had already been driven almost beyond its powers of endurance, to reach the fatal spot to save the seer's life.   Within a few paces of where the smoke was rising the poor brute could endure the strain no longer; it fell down under him and died on the spot. Still determined, if possible, to arrive in time, he rushed forward on foot, crying out at the height of his voice to those congregated at the spot, to save their victim.   It was, however, too late, for whether Seaforth's cries were heard or not, the victim of his lady's rage and vindictive nature had been thrown into the burning barrel a few moments before his intended deliverer had reached the fatal spot.

The time when this happened is not so very remote as to lead us to suppose that tradition could so grossly blunder as to record such a horrible and barbarous murder by a lady so widely and well-known as Lady Seaforth was, had it not taken place.

It is too much to suppose that if the seer had been allowed to die a peaceful and natural death, that such a story as this would have ever originated, be carried down and believed in from generation to generation, and be so well authenticated in many quarters as it now is.   It may be stated that a large stone slab, now covered under the sand, lies a few yards east from the road leading from Fortrose to Fort-George Ferry, and about 250 yards north-west from the lighthouse, which is still pointed out as marking the spot where this inhuman tragedy was consummated, under the eyes and with the full approval of the highest dignitaries of the Church.

THE FULFILMENT OF THE SEAFORTH
PROPHECY.

HAVING thus disposed of the seer himself, we next proceed to give in detail the fulfilment of the prophecies regarding the family of his cruel murderer. And we regret to say that the family of Seaforth will, in this connection, fall to be disposed of finally and for ever, and in the manner which Coinneach had unquestionably predicted. As already remarked, in due time the Earl returned to his home, after the fascinations of Paris had paled, and when he felt disposed to exchange frivolous or vicious enjoyment abroad for the exercise of despotic authority in the society of a jealous Countess at home. He was gathered to his fathers in 1678, and was succeeded by his eldest son, the fourth Earl. It is not our purpose to relate here the vicissitudes of the family which are unconnected with the curse of Coinneach Odhar, further than by giving a brief outline, though they are sufficiently remarkable to supply a strange chapter of domestic history.

The fourth Earl married a daughter of the illustrious family of Herbert, Marquis of Powis, and he himself was created a Marquis by the abdicated King of St. Germains, while his wife's brother was created a Duke. His son, the fifth Earl, having engaged in the rebellion of 1715, forfeited his estate and titles to the Crown; but in 1726 his lands were restored to him, and he, and his son after him, lived in wealth and honour as great Highland chiefs. The latter, who was by courtesy styled Lord Fortrose, represented his native county of Ross in several Parliaments about the middle of last century. In 1766, the honours of the peerage were restored to his son, who was created Viscount Fortrose, and in 1771, Earl of Seaforth; but those titles, which were Irish, did not last long, and became extinct at his death, in 1781. None of these vicissitudes were foretold in the seer's prophecy; and, in spite of them all, the family continued to prosper. That ruin which the unsuccessful rising in 1715 had brought upon many other great houses, was retrieved in the case of Seaforth, by the exercise of sovereign favour; and restored possessions and renewed honours preserved the grandeur of the race. But on the death of the last Earl, his second cousin, descended from a younger son of the third Earl and his vindictive Countess, inherited the family estates and the chiefdom of the Mackenzies, which he held for two short years, but never actually enjoyed, being slain at sea by the Mahrattas, at Gheriah, in the south of India, in 1783, after a gallant resistance. He was succeeded by his brother, in whom, as the last of his race, the seer's prophecy was accomplished.

Francis Humberston Mackenzie was a very remarkable man. He was born in 1794, and although deaf, and latterly dumb, he was, by the force of his natural abilities and the favour of fortune, able to fill an important position in the world. It would have been already observed that the " Last of the Seaforths " was born in full possession of all his faculties, and that he only became deaf from the effects of a severe attack of scarlet fever, while a boy in school, which we have previously noticed in connection with his remarkable dream. He continued to speak a little, and it was only towards the close of his life, and particularly during the last two years, that he was unable to articulate—or perhaps, unwilling to make the attempt, on finding himself the last male of his line. He may be said to have, prior to this, fairly recovered the use of speech, for he was able to converse pretty distinctly; but he was so totally deaf, that all communications were made to him by signs or in writing. Yet he raised a regiment at the beginning of the great European war; he was created a British peer in 1797, as Baron Seaforth of Kintail; in 1800 he went out to Barbadoes as Governor, and afterwards to Demerara and Berbice; and in 1808 he was made a Lieutenant-General. These were singular incidents in the life of a deaf and dumb man. He married a very amiable and excellent woman, Mary Proby, the daughter of a dignitary of the Church, and niece of the first Lord Carysfort, by whom he had a fine family of four sons and six daughters. When he considered his own position—deaf, and formerly dumb; when he saw his four sons, three of them rising to man's estate; and when he looked around him, and observed the peculiar marks set upon the persons of the four contemporary great Highland lairds, all in strict accordance with Coinneach's prophecy—he must have felt ill at ease, unless he was able, with the incredulous indifference of a man of the world, to spurn the idea from him as an old wife's superstition.

However, fatal conviction was forced upon him, and on all those who remembered the family tradition, by the lamentable events which filled his house with mourning. One after another his three promising sons (the fourth died young) were cut by death. The last, who was the most distinguished of them all, for the finest qualities both of head and heart, was stricken by a sore and lingering disease, and had gone, with a part of the family, for his health, to the

south of England.   Lord Seaforth remained in the north, at
Brahan Castle.   A daily bulletin was sent to him from the
sick chamber of his beloved son.   One morning, the
accounts being rather more favourable, the household began
to rejoice, and a friend in the neighbourhood, who was
visiting the chief, came down after breakfast full of the good
news, and gladly imparted it to the old family piper, whom
he met in front of the Castle.   The aged retainer shook his
head and sighed—" Na, na," said he, " he'll never recover.
It's decreed that Seaforth must outlive all his four sons."
This he said in allusion to the seer's prophecy; thus his
words were understood by the family; and thus members
of the family have again and again repeated the strange tale.
The words of the old piper proved too true.   A few more
posts brought to Seaforth the tidings of the death of the
last of his four sons.

At length, on the 11th January, 1815, Lord Seaforth died,
the last of his race.   His modern title became extinct.
The chiefdom of the Mackenzies, divested of its rank and
honour, passed away to a very remote collateral, who succeeded to no portion of the property, and the great Seaforth
estates were inherited by a white-hooded lassie from the
East.   Lord Seaforth's eldest surviving daughter, the
Honourable Mary Frederica Elizabeth Mackenzie, had
married, in 1804, Admiral Sir Samuel Hood, Bart., K.B.,
who was Admiral of the West India station while Seaforth
himself was Governor in those islands.   Sir Samuel afterwards had the chief command in the Indian seas, whither
his lady accompanied him, and spent several years with him
in different parts of the East Indies.   He died while holding
that high command, very nearly at the same time as Lord
Seaforth, so that his youthful wife was a recent widow at the
time, and returned home from India in her widow's weeds, to

take possession of her paternal inheritance. She was thus literally a white-coifed or white-hooded lassie (that is, a young woman in widow's weeds, and a Hood by name) from the East. After some years of widowhood, Lady Hood Mackenzie married a second time, Mr. Stewart, a grandson of the sixth Earl of Galloway, who assumed the name of Mackenzie, and established himself on his lady's extensive estates in the North. Thus, the possessions of Seaforth may be truly said to have passed from the male line of the ancient house of Mackenzie. And still more strikingly was this fulfilled, as regarded a large portion of these estates, when Mr. and Mrs. Stewart Mackenzie sold the great Island of Lewis to Sir James Matheson.

After many years of happiness and prosperity, a frightful accident threw the family into mourning. Mrs. Stewart Mackenzie was one day driving her younger sister, the Hon. Caroline Mackenzie, in a pony carriage, among the woods in the vicinity of Brahan Castle. Suddenly, the ponies took fright, and started off at a furious pace. Mrs. Stewart Mackenzie was quite unable to check them, and both she and her sister were thrown out of the carriage much bruised and hurt. She happily soon recovered from the accident, but the injury which her sister sustained proved fatal, and, after lingering for some time in a hopeless state, she died, to the inexpressible grief of all the members of her family. As Mrs. Stewart Mackenzie was driving the carriage at the time of the accident, she may be said to have been the innocent cause of her sister's death, and thus to have fulfilled the last portion of Coinneach's prophecy which has yet been accomplished.

Thus we have seen that the last chief of Seaforth was deaf and dumb ; that he had four sons ; that he survived them all ; that the four great Highland lairds who were his contemporaries were all distinguished by the peculiar personal marks the seer predicted ; that his estates were inherited by a white-coifed or white-hooded lassie from the East ; that his great possessions passed into the hands of other races ; and that his eldest daughter and heiress was so unfortunate as to be the innocent cause of her sister's death. In this very remarkable instance of family fate, the prophecy was not found out after the events occurred ; it had been current for generations in the Highlands, and its tardy fulfilment was marked curiously and anxiously by an entire clan and a whole county. Seaforth was respected and beloved far and near, and strangers, as well as friends and clansmen, mourned along with him the sorrows of his later years. The gradual development of the doom was watched with sympathy and grief, and the fate of Seaforth has been, during the last half-century of his life, regarded as one of the most curious instances of that second-sight for which the inhabitants of the Highlands of Scotland have been so long celebrated. Mr. Stewart Mackenzie, the accomplished husband of the heiress of Seaforth, after being for many years a distinguished member of the House of Commons and a Privy Councillor, held several high appointments in the Colonial Dominions of the British Crown. He was successively Governor of Ceylon and Lord High Commissioner of the Ionian Islands, and died, universally beloved and lamented, in the year 1843.

Lockhart in his *Life of Scott*, in reference to the Seaforth prediction, says :—" Mr. Morritt can testify thus far—that he heard the prophecy quoted in the Highlands at a time when Lord Seaforth had two sons alive, and in good health, and that it certainly was not made after the event ; " and he goes on to tell us that Scott and Sir Humphrey Davy were most certainly convinced of its truth, as also many others who had watched the latter days of Seaforth in the light of those wonderful predictions.

The late Duncan Davidson of Tulloch, Lord-Lieutenant of the County of Ross, on reading our Second edition, wrote to the author, under date of May 21, 1878, as follows :— " Many of these prophecies I heard of *upwards of seventy years ago, and when many of them were not fulfilled,* such as the late Lord Seaforth surviving his sons, and Mrs. Stewart-Mackenzie's accident, near Brahan, by which Miss Caroline Mackenzie was killed." Tulloch was, he said, during the latter years of Lord Seaforth, a regular visitor at Brahan Castle, and often heard the predictions referred to among members of the family. The letter is in our possession, and it was published, during Tulloch's life, and by his special permission, in Mackenzie's *History of the Mackenzies,* p. 267.

An attempt was recently made to sell the remaining possessions of the family, but fortunately, for the present, this attempt has been defeated by the interposition of the Marchioness of Tweeddale and Mrs. Colonel Stanley, daughters of the present nominal possessor of the property. At the time a leading article appeared in the *Edinburgh Daily Review* giving an outline of the family history of the Seaforths. After describing how the fifth Earl, with the fidelity characteristic of his house, " true as the dial to the sun," embraced the losing side in " the Fifteen ; " fought at the head of his clan at Sheriffmuir ; how in 1719 he, along with the Marquis of Tullibardine, and the Earl Marischal, made a final attempt to bring the " auld Stewarts back again ; " how he was dangerously wounded in an encounter with the Government forces at Glenshiel, and compelled to abandon the vain enterprise ; how he was carried on board a vessel by his clansmen, conveyed to the Western Isles, and ultimately to France ; how he was attainted by Parliament,

and his estates forfeited to the Crown ; how all the efforts of
the Government failed to penetrate into Kintail, or to collect
any rent from his faithful Macraes, whom the Seaforths had
so often led victorious from many a bloody conflict, from the
battle of Largs down to the Jacobite Rebellions of 1715 and
1719 ; and how the rents of that part of the estates were
regularly collected and remitted to their exiled chief in
France with a devotion and faithfulness only to be equalled
by their own countrymen when their beloved " bonnie
Prince Charlie " was a wanderer, helpless and forlorn, at the
mercy of his enemies, and with a reward of £30,000 at the
disposal of many a poverty-stricken and starving High-
lander, who would not betray his lawful Prince for all the
gold in England ; the article continues :—But their (the
Seaforth's) downfall came at last, and the failure of the male
line of this great historical family was attended with circumstances as singular as they were painful. Francis, Lord Seaforth, the last Baron of Kintail, was, says Sir Walter Scott,
" a nobleman of extraordinary talents, who must have made
for himself a lasting reputation, had not his political exertions been checked by painful natural infirmity." Though
deaf from his sixteenth year, and inflicted also with a partial
impediment of speech, he was distinguished for his attain-
ments as well as for his intellectual activity. He took a
lively interest in all questions of art and science, especially
in natural history, and displayed at once his liberality and
his love of art by his munificence to Sir Thomas Lawrence,
in the youthful straits and struggles of that great artist, and
by his patronage of other artists. Before his elevation to the
peerage, Lord Seaforth represented Ross-shire in Parliament for a number of years, and was afterwards Lord-
Lieutenant of the county. During the revolutionary war
with France, he raised a splendid regiment of Ross-shire

Highlanders (the 78th, the second which had been raised among his clan), of which he was appointed Lieutenant-Colonel Commandant, and he ultimately attained the rank of Lieutenant-General in the Army. He held for six years the office of Governor of Barbadoes, and, by his firmness and even-handed justice, he succeeded in putting an end to the practice of slave-killing, which at that time was not infrequent in the Island, and was deemed by the planters a venial offence, to be punished only by a small fine.

Lord Seaforth was the happy father of three (four) sons and six daughters, all of high promise ; and it seemed as if he were destined to raise the illustrious house of which he was the head, to a height of honour and power greater than it had ever yet attained. But the closing years of this nobleman were darkened by calamities of the severest kind. The mismanagement of his estates in the West Indies involved him in inextricable embarrassments, and compelled him to dispose of a part of his Kintail estates—" the gift-land " of the family, as it was termed—a step which his tenantry and clansmen in vain endeavoured to avert, by offering to buy in the land for him, that it might not pass from the family. He had previously been bereaved of two of his sons, and about the time that Kintail was sold, his only remaining son, a young man of talent and eloquence, the representative in parliament of his native county, suddenly died. The broken-hearted father lingered on for a few months, his fine intellect enfeebled by paralysis, and yet, as Sir Walter Scott says, " not so entirely obscured but that he perceived his deprivation as in a glass, darkly." Sometimes he was anxious and fretful because he did not see his son ; sometimes he expostulated and complained that his boy had been allowed to die without his seeing him ; and sometimes, in a less clouded state of intellect, he was

sensible of his loss in its full extent. The last " Cabarfeidh " followed his son to the grave in January, 1815, and
then—

> Of the line of Fitzgerald remained not a male,
> To bear the proud name of the Chiefs of Kintail.

The most remarkable circumstance connected with this
sorrowful tale, is the undoubted fact that, centuries ago, a
Seer of the Clan Mackenzie, known as Kenneth Oag (Odhar)
predicted that when there should be a deaf and dumb
" Cabarfeidh " (Staghead, the Celtic designation of the chief
of the clan, taken from the family crest), the "gift-land" of
their territory (Kintail) would be sold, and the male line
become extinct. This prophecy was well known in the
north long before its fulfilment, and was certainly not made
after the event. " It connected," says Lockhart, " the fall
of the house of Seaforth not only with the appearance of
a deaf ' Cabarfeidh,' but with the contemporaneous appearance of various different physical misfortunes in several of
the other great Highland chiefs, all of which are said to
have actually occurred within the memory of the generation
that has not yet passed away."

On the death of his lordship, his estates, with all their
burdens and responsibilities, devolved on his eldest daughter, Lady Hood, whose second husband was James Stewart
Mackenzie, a member of the Galloway family, and whose
son has just been prevented from selling all that remains of
the Seaforth estates. " Our friend, Lady Hood," wrote Sir
Walter Scott to Mr. Morritt, " will now be ' Cabarfeidh '
herself. She has the spirit of a chieftainess in every drop of
her blood, but there are few situations in which the cleverest
women are so apt to be imposed upon as in the management

of landed property, more especially of a Highland estate. I do fear the accomplishment of the prophecy that, when there should be a deaf ' Cabarfeidh,' the house was to fall." The writer concludes thus :—" Scott's apprehensions proved only too well founded. One section after another of the estates had to be sold. The remaining portion of Kintail, the sunny braes of Ross, the church lands of Chanonry, the barony of Pluscarden, and the Island of Lews—a principality itself—were disposed of one after the other, till now nothing remains of the vast estates of this illustrious house except Brahan Castle, and a mere remnant of their ancient patrimony (and that in the hands of trustees), which the non-resident, nominal owner has just been prevented from alienating. *Sic transit*."

Leaving these extraordinary prophecies with the reader, to believe, disbelieve, or explain away on any principle or theory which may satisfy his reason, his credulity, or scepticism, we conclude with the following :—

LAMENT FOR " THE LAST OF THE SEAFORTHS."

By Sir Walter Scott.

In vain the bright course of thy talents to wrong
Fate deaden'd thine ear and imprison'd thy tongue,
For brighter o'er all her obstructions arose
The glow of the genius they could not oppose ;
And who, in the land of the Saxon, or Gael,
Might match with Mackenzie, High Chief of Kintail ?

Thy sons rose around thee in light and in love,
All a father could hope, all a friend could approve ;
What 'vails it the tale of thy sorrows to tell ?
In the spring time of youth and of promise they fell !
Of the line of MacKenneth remains not a male,
To bear the proud name of the Chief of Kintail.

And thou, gentle Dame, who must bear, to thy grief,
For thy clan and thy country the cares of a Chief,
Whom brief rolling moons in six changes have left,
Of thy husband and father and brethren bereft ;
To thine ear of affection, how sad is the hail
That salutes thee—the heir of the line of Kintail !

Na 'm biodh an t'earball na bu ruighne bhiodh mo
sgialachd na b' fhaide.